Critical Success Factors in Enterprise Resource Planning Implementation in U.S. Manufacturing

by
Justin Lee Goldston, Ph.D.

COPYRIGHT 2019©

Dissertation Submitted in Partial Fulfillment of the Requirements for the Degree
of Doctor of Philosophy in Management, Walden University, February 2019

Author	Justin Lee Goldston, Ph.D.
Publisher	DBC Publishing, Sandston / Richmond, VA
ISBN	978-1-948149-09-9
Cover Art	2019© DBC Publishing

This text has been altered in format from the original dissertation to conform to better readability for the general-public and commercial publishing standards. The author may also have updated text, content, added more resources and bibliography material after the original dissertation was first published. Scholars reviewing the contents and formatting for thesis or dissertation styling should _not_ use this book's current *formatting* as a model. Please see your educational institution's established dissertation guidelines for the acceptable formatting for the graduate level thesis for research reporting.

Author:

You may contact the author with questions, comments, or continuing research inquiries at: justin.goldston@academiaworldwide.com

Table of Contents

List of Tables

List of Figures

For Sydney and Brooklyn

Abstract

A large number of failed Enterprise Resource Planning (ERP) implementations in recent years (2001-2016) makes these projects a risky endeavor for organizations of all sizes. Research regarding these critical failure factors was based on large enterprises, thus small- and medium-sized enterprises may be unable to implement the mitigation strategies suggested in those previous studies. A modified Delphi study with three rounds of iterative data collection and analysis from an expert panel of 42 manufacturing business consultants in the United States revealed a consensus on eight critical success factors in ERP implementations. The highest level of consensus as on desirability and feasibility for top management support and commitment, Enterprise Resource Planning fit with the organization, quality management, and a small internal team of the best employees.

Narrowing this gap of critical success factors contributed to positive social change by working toward building a consensus among ERP experts and scholars to improve project success and the triple-bottom-line for small- and medium-sized enterprises in the manufacturing industry. Because small- and medium-sized enterprises make up 99.7% of U.S. employer firms, gaining understanding on this business population was important given their constraints and limited prior research. The results of the study contribute to the fields of leadership and enterprise applications as the findings build on the body of knowledge for both disciplines.

Regardless of the size of the business organization, knowledge sharing is important, both upstream and downstream. Leaders can apply new knowledge within their organizations during times of change. Practitioners and subject matter experts in the ERP industry can apply the research identified during ERP implementations to mitigate risk and increase success during these ERP engagements.

Chapter 1

Introduction to the Study

Enterprise Resource Planning applications, also known as decision-support systems, are used by leaders of mid-to-large organizations to make financial and operational decisions. As companies continue to expand on a global scale, the need may grow for ERP applications to provide visibility, collaboration, and communication throughout their supply chains due to increased competition and customer demands. To minimize barriers and consequences when implementing change, leaders of organizations should devise a constructive approach (Al-Haddad & Kotnour, 2015). Although there may not be a universal managerial approach, managers should analyze their current business environment, reflect on the organization's strategic vision, and act on these issues many organizations currently face.

In the major sections of this chapter, the

researcher included the background of the study
followed by the need for the study based on the
problem the study addressed. The focus then moved
to the purpose of the study, the research question and
sub-questions, and the conceptual framework for the
study. The remaining sections included the nature of
the study, the definition of terms, assumptions, scope
and delimitations, and limitations. This chapter
included the significance of the study as it pertains to
the practice, to theory, and to positive social change.

Background of the Study

ERP applications were implemented in
manufacturing environments to provide operational
visibility throughout an organization's supply chain
network. With roughly 350,000 manufacturing
organizations in the United States as of the second
quarter of 2018, there was an increasing need to
identify ERP critical success factors as new
manufacturers entered the market and existing
manufacturers updated legacy systems (U.S.
Department of Labor, 2019). Researchers indicated
high-failure rates in ERP system implementations on

the metrics of budget, schedule overruns, and overall fit of planned business processes with implementation deliverables (Bintoro, Simatupang, Putro, & Hermawan, 2015; Ravasan & Mansouri, 2016; Shiri, Anvari, & Soltani, 2014). It was important to identify ways to mitigate these failures because of these high percentage of failure rates. Although Bansal and Agarwal (2015) used a small-sample size of ERP consultants to build a consensus on critical success factors in South Asian small- and medium-sized enterprises in their Delphi study, no Delphi study had focused on building a consensus using a large sample size of ERP consultants in the United States.

As the global market shrank with the rise in technological and logistical advances, leadership teams of organizations were looking for ways to make strategic decisions to maintain or increase their market share in their respective industries. In their research, Shao, Wang, and Feng (2015) found firms had turned to ERP systems to make operational, tactical, and strategic processes more efficient and effective. To provide additional background on ERP systems, Lin (2010) characterized ERP systems as an integrated, customized, and packaged software-based system that handled most system requirements in functional areas of a business such as finance, human resources, manufacturing, sales, and marketing. In addition to using ERP systems as a tool to make daily business decisions, these systems also could have been used as tools to improve knowledge sharing within the organization (Ifinedo & Olsen, 2014; Xie, Allen, & Ali, 2014). With ERP applications, organizational leaders enabled departments and facilities to share knowledge and collaborate instead of operating out of disparate systems.

Although empirical field experience had shown ERP systems affected businesses positively, the implementation and installation of these applications did come with potential risks. In one survey of 117 executives, 40% of the panelists stated their ERP projects failed to achieve their business case after one year of going live (Tsai, Li, Lee, & Tung, 2011). With the complexity of system functionalities, implementation and assimilation process was associated with high risk, leading to a high failure rate of ERP systems (Shao et al., 2015). With organizations of any kind and size increasingly adopting these systems to avoid technical obsolesce and create a sustainable competitive advantage (Maditinos, Chatzoudes, & Tsairidis, 2012), historically successful implementation strategies required further analysis to leverage these tools to potentially create a positive impact on social change for organizations, both internally and externally. The researcher focused on identifying a consensus among a panel of ERP manufacturing consultants as to the desirability and feasibility of critical success factors in ERP implementations in the United States in this study.

Problem Statement

Enterprise Resource Planning implementations cost organizations capital, human resources, and time. Although research on critical success factors in ERP implementations dated back to the 1970s (Rockart, 1979), a knowledge gap existed regarding critical success factors identified in the literature versus those applied in manufacturing environments (Deokar & Sarnikar, 2016; Khan, Nicho, & Takruri, 2016; Tarhini, Ammar, & Tarhini, 2015). Depending on the source or survey, researchers estimated between 70% and 85% of ERP implementations failed based on metrics such as cost, schedule overruns, or overall fit (Conteh & Akhtar, 2015; Ravasan & Mansouri, 2016; Sudhaman & Thangavel, 2015). Researchers have stated implementation failures cost large enterprises from $6M to $100M (USD) to implement (Conteh & Akhtar, 2015; Maas, Fenema, & Soeters, 2014; Mo & He, 2015). In extreme cases, companies filed for bankruptcy due to supply-chain disruptions attributed to ERP implementations (Haddara & Hetlevik, 2016; Joia, Macêdo, & Oliveira, 2014; Love, Matthews, Simpson, Hill, & Olatunji, 2014). With this level of investment and the expectation for operational optimization, it was important for business leaders to identify critical success factors integral to any ERP implementation.

The general problem was, despite a myriad of ERP implementation critical success factors identified in the academic and trade literature, implementation failures continued to occur at a high rate in the manufacturing industry (Hughes, Dwivedi, Rana, & Simintiras, 2016; Maas et al., 2014). Given the shift in managerial approaches, including the rise of partially distributed teams and other factors, the critical success factors previously noted in the literature may no longer have applied (Saade & Nijher, 2016). This study was important because the research on the interactions between ERP applications and positive social change were also lacking in academic and trade research (Grabski, Leech, & Schmidt, 2011). In performing a literature search on positive social change and ERP implementations, the researcher uncovered a gap that still existed on the research topic (Elbardan & Kholeif, 2017; Seth, Goyal, & Kiran, 2017).

The specific problem was – given the rise in complexity, adversity, and uncertainty across the manufacturing landscape – the desirability and feasibility of conventional ERP implementation critical success factors may have required reassessment among small- and medium-sized manufacturers (Alharthi, Alassafi, Walters, & Wills, 2017; Turner, Kutsch, & Leybourne, 2016). Due to increased competitiveness and customer expectations within the small- and medium-sized manufacturing sector, ERP implementation critical success factors should have been reviewed periodically for refinement (Rashid et al., 2018; Sharma, Dixit, & Qadri, 2015). What had been referred to as Industry 4.0 or the fourth industrial revolution, technological advancements had changed the way small- and medium-sized manufacturing organizations conduct business, creating paradigm shifts in organizational culture and leadership approaches (De Soete, 2016; Elkhani, Soltani, & Ahmad, 2014; Jackson, Nelson, & Proudfit, 2014). As small- and medium-sized manufacturers embraced the Internet of Things (IoT), future-oriented technologies triggered a requirement for leaders to develop lean, automated environments (Qin & Kai, 2016). The four industries that included healthcare, communication, and natural resources (e.g., food, water, and energy), and technology would have significantly affected the manufacturing industry over the next 10-15 years in forecasting global trends of the IoT (Basl, 2016). To remain competitive in respective business markets, manufacturing leaders were looking to ERP vendors and consultants to develop and deliver innovative products, services, and processes (Lasi, Fettke, Kemper, Feld, & Hoffmann, 2014; Qin & Kai, 2016). In performing an in-depth analysis of critical success factors implemented in the field, the researcher attempted to

narrow the scholar-practitioner gap by aligning the
most cited critical success factors in the literature with
those implemented during Industry 4.0.

Purpose of the Study

The purpose of this qualitative modified Delphi
study was to identify a consensus among an expert
panel of ERP manufacturing consultants for the
desirability and feasibility of critical success factors in
ERP implementations in the United States. The
purpose of a Delphi study was to acquire a reliable
consensus among a panel of experts through a series
of surveys (Habibi, Sarafrazi, & Izadyar, 2014; von
der Gracht & Darkow, 2013). The goal of this
research study was to reduce the scholar-practitioner
gap regarding critical success factors identified in the
literature versus those applied in manufacturing
environments. Reducing this gap may have
contributed to positive social change by working
toward a consensus among ERP manufacturing
consultants and scholars to improve project success
and the triple bottom line for organizations in the
manufacturing industry. Enterprise Resource

Planning applications could be an enabling factor in contributing to social change by providing firms with additional operational visibility, both internally and externally (Hassan & Mouakket, 2016). Sustainable ERP (S-ERP) applications could potentially provide solutions to support sustainable initiatives for an organization and its business environment (Chofreh et al., 2016). By integrating sustainable operations, processes, and information through knowledge-sharing within an organization, organizational leaders could potentially identify applications that could create a positive effect on social change by fostering employee collaboration, innovation, and empowerment.

Research Questions

This research study was undertaken to identify a consensus among a panel of ERP manufacturing consultants to identify the desirability and feasibility of critical success factors in ERP implementations in the United States. To provide a value justification and merit to the critical success factors identified in the literature, perceptions of desirability were selected for this study. To measure the practicality of the critical success factors identified in the literature, the perceptions of feasibility were selected for this study. The research question and sub-questions were:

RQ1- Qualitative: What is the level of consensus among ERP manufacturing consultants as to the desirability and feasibility of critical success factors for ERP implementations?

RQ1 Sub-question 1 - Qualitative: What is the level of consensus among ERP manufacturing consultants as to the desirability of critical success factors for ERP implementations?

RQ1 Sub-question 2 - Qualitative: What is the level of consensus among ERP manufacturing consultants as to the feasibility of critical success factors for ERP implementations?

Conceptual Framework

A conceptual framework constructed the structure of the study and served as a bridge between background theory and how the study was to be conducted in relation to other aspects that could have influenced the results of the study. The conceptual framework informed the design of the study and could have assisted in answering the research questions (Vrasidas & Zembylas, 2004). In qualitative research, researchers analyzed the data as it was collected from participants (Porter, 2011). To analyze participants' views effectively on critical success factors in small- and medium-sized manufacturers in the United States, a modified Delphi method was used to answer the research questions of this study.

To build a consensus among the critical success factors in ERP implementations, the critical success factor framework was the conceptual framework for this study. In the most cited study regarding critical success factors, Rockart (1979) defined critical success factors as competencies necessary to ensure successful performance.

As described in more detail in Chapter 2, the critical success factor framework was first introduced by Rubin and Seeling (1967) to analyze the effect of project managers in the success or failure of projects in the government sector. In response to this seminal study, Avots (1969) concluded project manager selection and leadership support were also critical success factors in project implementations. As the topic of critical success factors evolved, a number of researchers outlined critical success factors in projects as outlined in Figure 1.

Martin[30] (1976)	Locke[14] (1984)	Cleland and King[25] (1983)	Sayles and Chandler[28] (1971)	Baker, Murphy and Fisher[9] (1983)	Pinto and Slevin[7] (1989)	Morris and Hough[11] (1987)
Define goals	Make project commitments known	Project summary	Project manager's competence	Clear goals	Top management support	Project objectives
Select project organizational philosophy	Project authority from the top	Operational concept	Scheduling	Goal commitment of project team	Client consultation	Technical uncertainty innovation
General management support	Appoint competent project manager	Top management support	Control systems and responsibilities	On-site project manager	Personnel recruitment	Politics
Organize and delegate authority	Set up communications and procedures	Financial support	Monitoring and feedback	Adequate funding to completion	Technical tasks	Community involvement
Select project team	Set up control mechanisms (schedules, etc.)	Logistic requirements	Continuing involvement in the project	Adequate project team capability	Client acceptance	Schedule duration urgency
Allocate sufficient resources	Progress meetings	Facility support		Accurate initial cost estimates	Monitoring and feedback	Financial contract legal problems
Provide for control and information mechanisms		Market intelligence (who is the client)		Minimum start-up difficulties	Communication	Implement problems
Require planning and review		Project schedule		Planning and control techniques	Trouble-shooting	
		Executive development and training		Task (vs. social orientation)	Characteristics of the project team leader	
		Manpower and organization		Absence of bureaucracy	Power and politics	
		Acquisition			Environment events	
		Information and communication channels			Urgency	
		Project review				

Figure 1 - Seven lists of critical success factors developed in the literature.

Adapted from "A New Framework for Determining Critical Success/Failure Factors in Projects" by W. Belassi and O. I. Tukel, 1996, *International Journal of Project Management, 14*, p. 143. Copyright 1996 by Elsevier Science Ltd and IPMA.

Although Martin (1976) and Sayles and Chandler (1971) performed studies on benefits of information systems, their findings were too broad in scope regarding enterprise implementations (Belassi & Tukel, 1996). In studying complex systems such as ERP applications, researchers may consider analyzing all phases of these projects to create a manageable framework (Baxter & Sommerville, 2011). To address this gap in the research, Ho and Lin (2004) and Ngai, Cheng, and Ho (2004) created critical success factor frameworks for ERP implementations, as outlined in Figure 2. In their conclusions, Ho and Lin (2004) and Ngai et al. (2004) found that if leaders of organizations performed a systematic consideration of critical success factors during each phase of the implementation, the risk of project failure could be reduced.

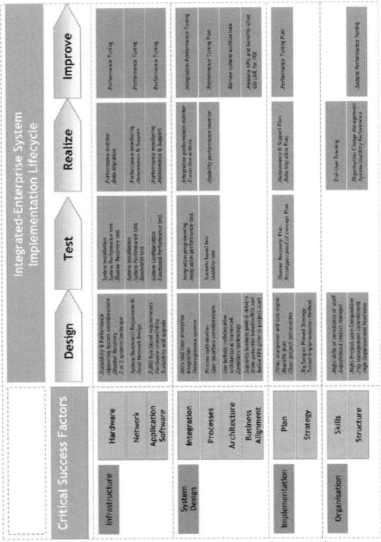

*Figure 2 - Integrated-enterprise system implementation
critical success factor framework reference matrix.*
Adapted from "Critical Success Factor Framework for the
Implementation of Integrated-Enterprise Systems in the
Manufacturing Environment" by L. T. Ho and G. C. I. Lin, 2004,
International Journal of Production Research, 42, p. 3736.
Copyright 2004 by Taylor and Francis Group, LLC.

Nature of the Study

A review of research methods conducted on
ERP implementations in small- and medium-sized
manufacturing environments was analyzed for this
study (Ngai, Law, & Wat, 2008; Remus & Wiener,
2010; Zeng, Wang, & Xu, 2015). After appraising
quantitative, qualitative, and mixed methods research
designs, the researcher selected a qualitative
approach and Delphi design.

To answer the research questions, qualitative
approaches were reviewed such as the grounded
theory, phenomenology, and the Delphi technique.
Although the grounded theory was a valuable
approach when collecting empirical research
(Eisenhardt, 1989; Orlikowski, 1993), the grounded
theory approach was not selected because the aim of
the study was not to develop a theory (Glaser &
Strauss, 2012). Because the goal of this study was to
establish a consensus to the desirability and feasibility
of critical success factor benchmarks for ERP
implementations, a phenomenological approach was
not chosen given its focus on exploring the essence

and meaning participants attach to the lived experience of a phenomenon (Moustakas, 1994). The Delphi method was selected for this study given its record as a good approach to anticipate long-term trends in technology (Adler & Ziglio, 1996; Linstone & Turoff, 2002).

The Delphi technique was a qualitative research design used to establish a consensus through the input from a panel of experts without the requirement of face-to-face interaction (Linstone & Turoff, 2002; von der Gracht & Darkow, 2013). Developed by Dalkey and Helmer at the RAND Corporation in 1953, the researchers were asked by the U.S. military to solicit expert opinion on selection of the optimal U.S. target system while also reducing the munitions output by establishing a prescribed number of atomic bombs (Brady, 2015; Dalkey & Helmer, 1963; Dalkey, Rourke, Lewis, & Snyder, 1972). In this study, the purpose of the Delphi approach was to predict a future outcome using expert opinions (Dalkey & Helmer, 1963; Dalkey et al., 1972).

The traditional Delphi technique consists of three rounds of surveys to reach a consensus. The typical panel size in a traditional Delphi study consists of between six to 12 experts (Habibi et al., 2014; Romano, 2010). Because the expert panel of consultants were asked to comment on existing critical success factors and propose modifications in the first round of the study, the approach was a modified study, as compared to a classical Delphi study. A modified Delphi approach was conducted because the Delphi study was designed with a target sample of 50 ERP manufacturing consultants to narrow a gap in the research and to align this study with the types of Delphi studies identified in the literature (Hung, Chang, Hung, Yen, & Chou, 2016; Zeng et al., 2015). This modified Delphi study was administered through SurveyMonkey. While there was no consensus among the implementation of critical success factors in the literature, using the Delphi method helped to find a consensus as to the desirability and feasibility of critical success factors in ERP implementations in the United States.

This Delphi study involved three rounds of data collection and analysis. In the first round, the expert panel of ERP manufacturing consultants were asked to comment on the existing critical success factors outlined in Figure 4 in Chapter 3 the panelists thought were most desirable and to propose any modifications they could offer. Focusing on the desirability and modifications in Round 1 was noted as an acceptable and common approach in modified Delphi studies (Elnasr, Sobaih, Ritchie, & Jones, 2012; Hsu & Sandford, 2007). After reviewing the responses, the top 10 most desirable critical success factors with the highest frequency were moved to Round 2 of the study. To provide a value justification and merit to the critical success factors identified in the literature, perceptions of desirability were selected for this study. To measure the practicality of the critical success factors identified in the literature, the perceptions of feasibility were selected for this study.

In Round 2 the panelists rated the desirability and feasibility of the critical success factors using a Likert-type scale. The critical success factors with the highest ratings of desirability and feasibility in Round 2 were moved to Round 3, during which the ERP manufacturing consultants rated the remaining critical success factors for desirability and feasibility. Subsequent rounds of rating were not required as consensus was reached in Round 3.

To determine the level of consensus, researchers identified that when 75% of experts selected a four or five on a Likert-type scale, consensus had been met (Diamond et al., 2014; Fox et al., 2016; Paoloni et al., 2017). In the current research study, a four pertained to desirable or feasible; a five pertained to highly desirable or highly feasible. In performing this methodical approach, the researcher attempted to narrow the gap between the critical success factors identified in the literature versus the critical success factors employed in the field of ERP consulting.

Definitions

Terms in the industry, as well as in academia, can take on different meanings. Because definitions conflict in certain disciplines, defining the terms in this study was essential. This section outlined the terms used in this study as each pertains to ERP implementations.

Blockchain: A blockchain is a distributed public ledger collectively kept up to date according to strict rules and general agreement. Blockchain enables all parties to reach a consensus in a system with potentially malicious actors without a central authority (Dai & Vasarhelyi, 2017; Hofmann & Rüsch, 2017).

Business process reengineering (BPR): The business process reengineering process is the modification of business processes and procedures to increase operational efficiencies within an organization (Mitra & Mishra, 2016).

Change management: Change management within an organization involves planning, developing, and implementing internal initiatives to transition from current state to future state processes (Zhang, Schmidt, & Li, 2016).

Critical failure factors (CFFs): Critical failure factors are the metrics and processes during an ERP implementation where things go wrong, resulting in failure to meet project expectations (Malaurent & Avison, 2015; Ravasan & Mansouri, 2016).

Critical success factors (CSFs): Critical success factors within an implementation are the operational strategies, practices, and tools believed to lead to the successful adoption and installation of ERP applications (Fayaz, Kamal, Amin, & Khan, 2017; Ram & Corkindale, 2014).

Desirability: Desirability in ERP implementations is the added value or significance of deploying the critical success factor in the implementation project (Ludlow & Blackham, 2015).

ERP: Enterprise Resource Planning applications are information systems packages that integrate all of the business functions of an organization into one core application (Gajic, Stankovski, Ostojic, Tesic, & Miladinovic, 2014; Ravasan & Mansouri, 2016; Shen, Chen, & Wang, 2016).

Feasibility: Feasibility within an ERP implementation is the likelihood a strategy, process, or tool will be successfully implemented within a project (Day & Bobeva, 2005; Steurer, 2011).

Fourth industrial revolution: Also referred to as Industry 4.0, the fourth industrial revolution is an initiative adopted by the manufacturing industry to use technology such as big-data analytics, the Internet of Things (IOT), cloud computing, and robotics to streamline processes, reduce operating costs, and improve employee environments (Qin & Kai, 2016).

Go live: An ERP go live is an established cut-over date when end users move from an organization's legacy application and use the full features of the new ERP application (Abdinnour & Saeed, 2015; Li, Chang, & Yen, 2017).

Implementation: An implementation is a project an organization undertakes composed of a variety of phases such as acquisition, design, implementation, stabilization, and transformation phases (Bansal & Agarwal, 2015; Ravasan & Mansouri, 2016).

Information systems (IS): Information systems are a set of interrelated applications that store and retrieve information to support decision-making activities across all departments within an organization (Hu, Pedrycz, Wang, & Wang, 2016).

Knowledge sharing (KS): Knowledge sharing is the process through which one organizational unit is affected by the experience of another as an event through which one entity learns from the experience of another (Rezania & Ouedraogo, 2013).

Large enterprises (LE): Large enterprises are organizations that employ more than 500 employees in the United States (Amba & Abdulla, 2014).

Legacy systems: Legacy systems are existing information technology applications used to operate business processes that firms look to replace with new ERP solutions (Conteh & Akhtar, 2015).

Modules: Modules are sub-areas of an ERP application such as finance, purchasing, warehouse management, and sales that firms can implement in a phased approach during the implementation (Amba & Abdulla, 2014).

Project scope: The project scope is defined as the required tasks or modules that should be implemented to ensure ERP project success (Orouji,

2016). Some implementations will split projects into different phases with each having a detailed scope.

Small- and medium-sized enterprises (SMEs): Small- and medium-sized enterprises are organizations that employ less than 500 employees in the United States (Amba & Abdulla, 2014).

Stakeholders: Stakeholders are individuals and organizations directly and indirectly affected by an ERP implementation (Saade & Nijher, 2016). Stakeholders include executive leadership, managers, supervisors, employees, vendors, and customers (Carvalho & Guerrini, 2017; Huang, 2016).

Super users: Super users are individuals and resources on the implementation team assigned to learn the processes and procedures of the new ERP application, and train co-workers and subordinates on the new processes (Mahdavian, Wingreen, & Ghlichlee, 2016).

Triple bottom line: The triple bottom line is defined as the economic, social, and environmental intentions of corporate responsibility and measures the organization's sustainability (Glavas & Mish, 2015).

Assumptions

This qualitative, modified Delphi study included several assumptions necessary for the modified Delphi study. These assumptions were not exhaustive, but they assisted in framing the study. Based on the criteria to compose an expert panel of ERP manufacturing consultants with at least five years of ERP implementation experience in the manufacturing industry, the first assumption was the participants who self-selected into the study were knowledgeable in the field. Another assumption was the participants would respond to the survey questions based on empirical experience in ERP manufacturing implementations and would not be influenced by the nature of the questions or by outside sources or individuals. A third assumption was a sufficient number of ERP manufacturing consultants were willing to participate in each round of the study given the pool of available ERP manufacturing consultants were solicited through the

LinkedIn online platform. The fourth assumption was the ERP manufacturing consultants would respond openly and honestly to the survey questions because of their own experience and interest in the research topic.

Another assumption was, early on, some participants could drop out of the study due to the nature of a Delphi approach. To mitigate this risk to maintain sufficient retention through all rounds to achieve a consensus, each participant in the study was selected based on meeting criteria about tenure in the industry. The study involved a mitigation strategy to encourage participants in the first round to complete all subsequent rounds. By sending reminders to all members of the initially-targeted participants through LinkedIn before and during each round, a sufficient number of participants was attained.

The final assumption was the appropriateness of the modified Delphi technique to answer the research question and execution of this approach with fidelity based on the foundations outlined by previous researchers (Habibi et al., 2014; von der Gracht & Darkow, 2013).

Scope and Delimitations

In establishing the scope of this study, three primary criteria were considered: what to study, who to study, and requirements for the sample size. With firms continuing to implement ERP solutions that failed to meet expectations amid extensive research, additional examination was required to mitigate ERP implementation risk. A controlled vocabulary search on Google Scholar of ERP critical success factors returned 24,400 results. Researchers estimated between 70% and 85% of ERP implementations continue to fail based on metrics such as cost, schedule overruns, or overall fit (Conteh & Akhtar, 2015; Ravasan & Mansouri, 2016; Sudhaman & Thangavel, 2015). With ERP implementations carrying this high level of risk, proven critical success factors practiced in the past were reviewed to analyze aspects and factors of desirability and feasibility in future implementations.

To reduce bias in creating the selection criteria for participants in the current research study, pertinent academic and trade literature influenced the identification of which expertise and experience was required. Studies revealed project managers provided insight throughout each phase of the implementation (Mahdavian et al., 2016), while other findings supported a stronger case with ERP consultants in revealing consultants had greater influence on project success through their approach on establishing future state processes and procedures (Sudhaman & Thangavel, 2015). By selecting ERP consultants from a number of ERP providers, the results of this reserach study would have been transferable across ERP platforms and implementation methodologies.

Based on the requirements for ERP consultants in a study focusing on small and medium manufacturers, the participants in the study were consultants who had implemented ERP solutions in the manufacturing industry. Given the premise of the Delphi technique to establish a consensus through the input from a panel of experts, the ERP manufacturing consultants had a minimum of five years of experience in implementing ERP solutions in the manufacturing industry. Because ERP research has been focused on large enterprises (Conteh &

Akhtar, 2015; Maas et al., 2014; Mo & He, 2015), the researcher focused on small- and medium-sized enterprises. The researcher focused only on critical success factors deployed during ERP implementations within manufacturers in the United States. With the different cultures, processes, and procedures applied in United States' small- and medium-sized manufacturers as compared to other parts of the world, the results of this study may not have been applicable in other countries.

Limitations

The limitations outlined in this study were common to studies with a qualitative Delphi research approach. Limitations were identified as situations that were out of the researcher's control. Due to the nature of the Delphi study, some ERP manufacturing consultants dropped out of the study during each of the rounds. There was a possibility of a low response rate in this study. Time requirements were also a limitation in this study. One drawback to a Delphi study was that several days or weeks could have passed due to the analysis and collection of surveys

(Aengenheyster et al., 2017). Because of the time-lapse in data collection and analysis, the risk of consultant-participant attrition could arise due to time constraints or scheduling conflicts (Gray, 2016; McMillan, King, & Tully, 2016). The researcher allocated a week-long period to allow sufficient time for data analysis. The data were analyzed within 24-hours, relying on analysis tools within the SurveyMonkey survey platform and Statistical Package for the Social Sciences (SPSS) statistical software.

Although the sampling criteria included ERP manufacturing consultants with at least five years of experience implementing ERP solutions, the participants could have had varying levels of expertise and experience. Because some consultants may not have possessed the in-depth knowledge of some of the critical success factors identified in the survey, an uneven distribution of experience could have been represented in the results (Hsu & Sandford, 2007). To minimize this uneven distribution, the study involved a purposive sampling technique to ensure meaningful results in the study. Screening questions at the beginning of the survey ensured participants had the minimum-required expertise and experience based on the identified population sample.

Another limitation in this research study was of researcher bias. Given the researcher had a decade of experience implementing ERP applications in small- and medium-sized manufacturing environments, the selection of participants was potentially inherent. There was the possibility the researcher may have known the ERP consultants' participating in the study, and thus the researcher may have had preconceptions before the study was conducted (Hasson, Keeney, & McKenna, 2000; Okoli & Pawlowski, 2004). Although purposive sampling was used to obtain expert panelists with required expertise and experience, this approach could have been viewed as a strength of the study (Elledge & McAleer, 2015). In addressing the limitation of response bias, some bias and assumptions could have played a factor in the results. Response bias may have arisen when panelists provided an expected answer in each round of a Delphi study (Elledge & McAleer, 2015).

The minimum recommended response rate for each round was between 40% and 50% (Atkinson &

Gold, 2001). An initial target group of 125 consultants were invited to participate in the research study to reach the projected sample size of 50 consultants, in preparation of a Round 1 response rate range of 48% to 74% (Mokkink et al., 2010) and potential attrition in later rounds (Hasson et al., 2000; Hsu & Sandford, 2007). Because study participants should have had first-hand experience in implementing ERP applications, the results of this research study should reach more realistic expectations.

The critical success factors in this study were limited to those identified by Saade and Nijher (2016) in their research. Although the Round 1 survey included definitions of each critical success factor, a limitation was the potential for the ERP manufacturing consultants to have had inaccurate perceptions of the critical success factors due to naming conventions used in their respective business environments. To counter inaccurate perceptions, the researcher performed a field test with definitions added to one metric (based on expert feedback to ensure participants fully understood the critical success factor) when taking the survey. In performing a research study on small- and medium-sized manufacturers in the United States, the results of the study may not be generalizable to different populations, industries, or geographical regions.

Significance of the Study

The researcher's aim for this study was to provide a blueprint to implement ERP applications successfully for both scholars and practitioners. To complete this task, a Delphi study was performed with panelists regarded in the ERP industry as the experts – the consultants (Bansal & Agarwal, 2015; Bronnenmayer, Wirtz, & Göttel, 2016a; Chang, Wang, Jiang, & Klein, 2013). The identification of critical success factors in the ERP consulting community was subjective due to empirical evidence of implementing these applications in various environments (Sun, Ni, & Lam, 2015).

Failed traditional ERP applications focused on the profitability aspect of an organization, whereas sustainable ERP (S-ERP) applications were focused on aspects the triple bottom line (TBL) (Bintoro et al., 2015; Chofreh, Goni, Shaharoun, Ismail, & Klemeš, 2014; Malaurent & Avison, 2015). Chofreh et al.

(2016) posited that S-ERP systems are based on people, planet, and profit, which in turn will have created a collaborative, synergistic, sustainable environment for business partners and communities. With the increase in collaboration and strategic relationships between business partners, a demand to support these organizational systems will have spurred firms to increase their operational workforces, resulting in a positive impact to communities around the world.

In addition to the positive effect to a firm's TBL, this research study may contribute to positive social change by reducing the risk of inadvertently implementing an unprofitable ERP solution. For ERP vendors, this research study may have assisted in educating, certifying, and employing additional members of their operational workforce through the successful delivery of consulting services (Bronnenmayer, Wirtz, & Göttel, 2016b). The results of this research study could provide valid a foundation for educational and training programs (Denzin & Lincoln, 2005). This research approach could potentially be beneficial for ERP vendors to provide a reliable and validated education plan that could assist in successfully onboarding new hires, as well as potentially instilling a continuous improvement process to ensure tenured consultants were aligned with current technological developments. The results of this research study may have contributed to positive social change by mitigating the risk of failed ERP implementations by outlining a forward-looking view of critical success factors through the lens of ERP manufacturing consultants (given the consultant's subject matter expertise in the field).

Significance to Practice

In ERP implementations, researchers stated consultants were integral to the success of the project (Ravasan & Mansouri, 2016; Sudhaman & Thangavel, 2015; Tsai, Lin, Chen, & Hung, 2007). Because ERP providers who supported the manufacturing industry focused on niche markets, selecting ERP manufacturing consultants from various ERP vendors could potentially provide a broader view of critical success factors for this industry. Enterprise Resource Planning implementations could cost business organizations hundreds of thousands of dollars (USD)

in capital and resource hours. The researcher
conducted this study to identify the critical success
factors that could potentially mitigate the risk in these
projects.

Deploying critical success factors in ERP
implementations could lead to a strategic competitive
advantage, with the risk mitigation strategies (Forcht,
Kieschnick, Aldridge, & Shorter, 2007; Habibzadeh,
Meshkani, & Shoshtari, 2016). By using the
capabilities of ERP applications, leaders of
organizations could have improved operational
efficiencies and enhanced their supply chain visibility,
resulting in a competitive differentiation (Ghosh &
Biswas, 2017; Ram, Wu, & Tagg, 2014).

Significance to Theory

Enterprise Resource Planning applications
were first established in the 1970s, but organizations
continued to grow in the number of plants, size of
workforce, complexity of products, and production
capabilities. With project teams continuing to
experience failed ERP implementations, it was
important for leaders within organizations to

understand how IT and business synergized to
increase operational efficiencies and profitability
(Chen, 2010). Although research (1967 – 2019) on
ERP critical success factors had focused on a limited
amount of case studies on small and medium
manufacturers, a limited amount of research had
included consultants as the sample population.
Because ERP manufacturing consultants were
viewed as subject matter experts, both from an IT and
best business practice perspective (Bansal &
Agarwal, 2015; Chang et al., 2013), the results of this
study may have contributed to the theoretical body of
knowledge. In producing the results of this research
project, the scholar-practitioner gap may be narrowed
by identifying, reviewing, and implementing the top
critical success factors in this study.

Significance to Social Change

To identify a consensus among a panel of ERP
manufacturing consultants, the future-oriented
approach of the modified Delphi technique may have
contributed to positive social change by having
improved efficiencies and work environments for

employees in small- and medium-sized manufacturing firms in the United States. The results of this qualitative modified Delphi study may have contributed to the ERP body of knowledge by revealing consensus about the critical success factors of implementations in small- and medium-sized manufacturers in the United States. Positive social change occurred when ERP providers and users created a positive impact on the industrial sectors they served, educated, and certified (Lin, Ma, & Lin, 2011). This research study's results and conclusions may provide beneficial information for leaders of organizations, as well as ERP vendors, for use through each phase of future implementations. Application of the results of this study could also have improved the implementation methodologies of ERP providers and increased the probability of successful ERP implementations by mitigating risks that could arise during the implementation life cycle by having instituted the outlined critical success factors.

The findings of this research study may also have had the potential to influence business success. Positive social change within ERP implementations may have enhanced employee knowledge, critical

thinking skills, and organizational collaboration (Al-
Johani & Youssef, 2013; Le Pennec & Raufflet, 2016).
Enterprise Resource Planning applications provided a
sustainable competitive advantage to organizations
by empowering employees to share ideas and
promote job stability (Azevedo, Romão, & Rebelo,
2014; Beheshti, Blaylock, Henderson, & Lollar, 2014).
In implementing ERP applications, leaders promoted
positive social change by providing additional job
opportunities and higher wages through the increased
efficiencies ERP applications provided within an
organization (Gajic et al., 2014; Pishdad, Koronios,
Reich, & Geursen, 2014).

Summary and Transition

Enterprise Resource Planning applications
integrated systems that centralized processes,
information, and data from departments and/or sites
within an organization. Project teams implemented
applications to gain visibility across supply chains,
improve operational efficiencies, and align strategic
objectives of shareholders (Chen, Harris, Lai, & Li,
2016; Yassien, 2017). The problem was ERP

implementation failures continued at a high rate in the manufacturing industry despite the critical success factors identified in the literature (Hughes et al., 2016; Maas et al., 2014). The purpose of this qualitative modified Delphi study was to identify a consensus among a panel of ERP manufacturing consultants as to the desirability and feasibility of critical success factors in ERP implementations in the United States.

The research methodology was a qualitative modified Delphi approach. Based on the conceptual framework, the critical success factor framework was reviewed to answer the research question outlined above. By identifying a consensus among a subject matter expert panel of ERP manufacturing consultants, the results may have provided a blueprint to implement ERP applications successfully for both academic scholars and practitioners.

Chapter 2

Literature Review

Enterprise Resource Planning applications were tools leaders used to make managerial decisions and provide visibility throughout their business organizations. Although studies outlined benefits of implementing these applications, researchers also noted these projects were considered a risky endeavor for organizations of all sizes (Abdelmoniem, 2016; Bansal & Agarwal, 2015; Shao et al., 2015). Costs of ERP implementations ranged from 1-3% of an organization's annual revenue and could have lasted, on average, one to three years (Stanciu & Tinca, 2013). With small- and medium-sized enterprises (SMEs), these risks and expenditures were further amplified because of limited resources, expertise, and budgets. Such external risks could have led SMEs to delay the project of ERP implementation or forego it altogether. Internally,

SMEs may have found it difficult to implement re-engineering projects due to limited resources. Overall, SMEs may have faced greater challenges in adopting technology as compared to large enterprises, given the constraints mentioned (Ghobakhloo, Hong, Sabouri, & Zulkifli, 2012). Ghobakhloo et al.'s research findings supported the imperativeness of focusing this research study on ERP implementations in small and medium manufacturing environments.

The definition of ERP systems was derived from the top researchers in recent years (2014-2016) as information systems packages that integrated the business functions of an organization into one core application (Gajic et al., 2014; Ravasan & Mansouri, 2016; Shen et al., 2016). In addition to this characterization, ERP applications could have brought disparate systems into one application in an attempt to create a synergistic environment within the organization. The size of these projects supported the importance of focusing on SMEs to identify metrics that could have enabled the organization to become successful in the endeavor. Large enterprises could have utilized large budgets and pools of experienced resources for an ERP implementation. Subject matter experts could have been constrained in their support to large implementations from limited capital and human resources (Bansal & Agarwal, 2015; Mittal, 2016). Subject matter experts were represented by a range of inherent characteristics that distinguished them from large enterprises, such as ownership type, structure, culture, and market (Zach & Munkvold, 2012). To mitigate risks of ERP implementations, scholars must have educated practitioners of these manufacturing environments of critical success factors (CSFs) that were identified from previous successful implementations.

In reviewing the literature on CSFs in ERP implementations, factors were identified that contributed to the success of ERP implementations. Few of these CSFs were technological in nature (Ravasan & Mansouri, 2016). A review of the literature on ERP systems revealed studies regarding CSFs and critical failure factors (CFFs) implemented by small- and medium-sized enterprises engaging in ERP implementations. The aim of this research was to identify a consensus among a panel of ERP manufacturing consultants as to the desirability and feasibility of CSFs in ERP implementations in the United States.

The research question and sub-questions were as follows:

RQ1: What is the level of consensus among ERP manufacturing consultants as to the desirability and feasibility of critical success factors for ERP implementations?

RQ1 Sub-question 1: What is the level of consensus among ERP manufacturing consultants as to the desirability of critical success factors for ERP implementations?

RQ1 Sub-question 2: What is the level of consensus among ERP manufacturing consultants as to the feasibility of critical success factors for ERP implementations?

Conceptual Framework

The acceleration of globalization and collaboration among business partners resulted in a need for leaders of organizations to increase visibility and collaboration. Through the use of enterprise applications, leaders were able to make this vision a reality. To build a consensus among the critical success factors in ERP implementations, the use of a conceptual framework blended the empirical experience of ERP manufacturing consultants with conceptual conclusions from academic literature (Berman, 2013; Leshem & Trafford, 2007; Smith, Bonacina, Kearney, & Merlat, 2000). The conceptual framework for this research study was developed from the critical success factors related to project success based on the findings of Avots (1969), Belassi and Tukel (1996), Ho and Lin (2004), Ngai et al. (2004), Rockart (1979), Rubin and Seeling (1967), and Saade and Nijher (2016).

Rubin and Seeling (1967) were the first researchers to study the complexities of the interactions between systems, people, and processes and introduced critical success factors when they analyzed the impact of project managers in the success or failure of projects within the government sector. Rubin and Seeling concluded that – although the experience of the project manager had no impact on project success – the size of previous projects did affect a project manager's performance. In another study, Avots (1969) concluded leadership support was integral to the success of projects. Leadership support was a critical success factor for which researchers had reached a consensus (Baxter & Sommerville, 2011; Belassi & Tukel, 1996; Cleland & King, 1983). As researchers shifted the critical success factor framework to ERP implementations, Ho and Lin (2004) and Ngai et al. (2004) found if leaders of organizations performed a systematic consideration of critical success factors during each phase of the implementation, the risk of project failure could have been reduced.

Project sponsors, team members, and stakeholders should have collaborated to ensure project success in applying the critical success factor framework within ERP implementations (Dwivedi et al., 2015; Giachetti, 2016). As global expansion and

customer expectations continued to increase, leaders
of organizations implemented enterprise applications
to remain competitive (Gupta, Aye, Balakrishnan,
Rajagopal, & Nguwi, 2014; Zughoul, Al-Refai, & El-
Omari, 2016). Using the right tools and approaches
made the job easier … while using the wrong
approaches made the job difficult. A literature search
in Google Scholar for most cited article, identified a
study regarding critical success factors, Rockart
(1979) identified and defined critical success factors
as competencies necessary to ensure successful
performance. Transferring the knowledge identified in
previous studies, this research study was able to
identify and combine viewpoints and perspectives
from ERP manufacturing consultants to reach a
consensus for desirability and feasibility of identified
critical success factors in ERP implementations in the
United States.

Identified as one of the most important
business innovations (Zughoul et al., 2016), ERP
systems streamlined complex business cases for
organizations around the world (Fu-Long, Lei, & Ji-
Hong, 2017). To mitigate risks of ERP projects,
leaders implemented a combination of knowledge,

skills, and individual characteristics identified as
critical success factors within framework studies to
ensure project success (Müller & Turner, 2007).
Manufacturing leaders of large-, medium-, and small-
sized organizations implemented ERP solutions to
integrate complex processes such as supply chain
management, customer service, engineering,
purchasing, and finance. The objective of these
projects was to increase the collaboration and
visibility throughout the organization's supply chain
network.

During times of change, including ERP
implementations, uncertainty, and risk were inherent
(Bintoro et al., 2015; Zeng et al., 2015). How project
teams implemented these projects could have had
positive or negative effects on organizational
performance (Akca & Ozer, 2014; Chien, Lin, & Shih,
2014). Studies focused on the critical success factor
framework within ERP implementations resulted in
identifying project team activities as critical success
factors in research findings (Ho & Lin, 2004; Ngai et
al., 2004; Saade & Nijher, 2016). Given ERP success
can be difficult to measure (Abelein & Paech, 2013;
Althonayan & Althonayan, 2017), the use of a critical

success factor framework may have provided a better
measure of an ERP implementation's success. The
critical success factor framework was selected for the
current research study given this conceptual
framework had been validated, challenged, and
adopted to measure success in Information Systems
projects (Ho & Lin, 2004; Ngai et al., 2004).

Literature Review

Enterprise applications were complex
architectures that assisted leaders of organizations in
making tactical and strategic business decisions.
Studies identified in the literature review investigated
the history of ERP systems, the future of enterprise
applications, implementation success, ERP
implementations in small- and medium-sized
manufacturing environments, and managerial
approaches during times of organizational change.
This research study analyzed and synthesized the
literature as it pertained to enterprise applications.

The Evolution of Enterprise Applications

As computers were introduced in the 1960s, organizations developed applications to track inventory, assist in ordering materials, and created data related to produce and finished goods. In a concept identified as inventory control, firms took the first step in systematically running the operational side of an organization (Jacobs & Weston, 2007; Thakur, 2016). In the 1970s, Materials Requirements Planning (MRP) applications were introduced to enable manufacturers to enable purchase decisions, create forecasts, and schedule production, spawning the founding firms of the industry such as SAP and J. D. Edwards (Egdair, Rajemi, & Nadarajan, 2015; Jacobs & Weston, 2007; Singh & Nagpal, 2014). With the number of organizations creating additional requirements to reduce business overhead costs, J. D. Edwards enhanced their proprietary MRP applications to include closed-loop scheduling, enhanced shop-floor reporting, and forward scheduling known as MRP-II (Jacobs & Weston, 2007; Kumar & Van Hillegersberg, 2000). As

organizational leaders began to revert to technology
to assist in daily operational decision-making, by the
end of the 1980s, the primary ERP vendors were
established as go-to sources: SAP, IBM, J. D.
Edwards, Baan, PeopleSoft, and Oracle (Razzhivina,
Yakimovich, & Korshunov, 2015). Enterprise
applications enabled decision-makers to provide
better visibility of inventory and production levels;
organizations also looked to these applications to set
themselves apart from their business competition.

In the 1990s, with the market becoming
competitive, the major business players looked for a
competitive advantage. These business entities
released applications that integrated organizational
operations within the accounting department functions
(Bhuiyan, Chowdhury, & Ferdous, 2014). Coined as
"ERP" by the Gartner Group, this new technological
development spurred growth within the core of six
business application vendors: (a) Systemanalyse und
Programmentwicklung (SAP; English translation is
Systems, Applications & Program Development); (b)
J. D. Edwards; (c) PeopleSoft; (d) Oracle; (e)
International Business Machines (IBM); and, (f) Baan
(Jacobs & Weston, 2007). With the fear of the

unknown approaching for the year 2000 with Y2K, ERP industry marketing caused firms to scramble to install these applications, sparking dramatic growth in ERP vendors and offerings (Brumberg et al., 2016; Salimi, Dankbaar, & Davidrajuh, 2015). When the dot-com bubble of 2000 rocked the entire technology industry, the major players in the industry were pressured to downsize (Fadlalla & Amani, 2015). By the end of the 2000s, the ERP landscape changed as J. D. Edwards, and PeopleSoft were acquired by Oracle (Palanisamy, Verville, & Taskin, 2015) and a new entrant in the market, Infor Global Solutions acquired Baan (Verdouw, Robbemond, & Wolfert, 2015) and IBM's Manufacturing, Accounting and Production Information Control Systems (MAPICS) product (Banerjee, 2015), resulting in SAP, Oracle, and Infor becoming the top three ERP vendors in the market, respectively.

In reaching the maturity stage of its lifecycle, ERP applications continued to progress with a gradual introduction of cloud computing. Cloud computing reduces the information technology (IT) overhead for firms by moving hardware to support its ERP application off premise to a vendor-hosted site

(Bento, Bento, & Bento, 2015). In a 2016 ERP report performed by Panorama Consulting, the survey of 215 organizations deploying ERP applications uncovered a 40% increase in firms implementing cloud-based versus on-premise solutions compared to 2015 (Solutions, 2016). Reduced misconceptions of cloud computing led to an increase in the adoption of cloud solutions (Solutions, 2016). As ERP providers continued to increase application security to mitigate the risk of security breaches, more organizations moved from on-premise solutions to cloud-based vendors and packages.

In addition to cloud computing, to reduce waste within operations, the supply chain community instituted Lean Six Sigma initiatives over the past two decades (2001-2018), which were also integrated into ERP applications (De Soete, 2016). Researchers called these new applications Sustainable Enterprise Resource Planning (S-ERP) applications. The premise of this chapter focused on how S-ERPs could have positively impacted aspects of an organization's TBL, as well as global sustainability. Refer to Table 1 for a graphical representation of the evolution of business applications.

Table 1 - The Evolution of Business Applications

Decade	Applications
1960s	Early computers, Reorder point systems, and early Materials Requirements Planning (MRP)
1970s	MRP
1980s	MRPII and early Enterprise Resource Planning (ERP)
1990s	ERP
2000s	Introduction to ERP cloud computing, early ERP vendor consolidations, mergers, and acquisitions
The future	Sustainable Enterprise Resource Planning (S-ERP)

The Birth of S-ERP

As firms became more innovative and socially conscious, leaders utilized technology to integrate sustainable operations, processes, and information through knowledge-sharing within the business organization. Sustainable development and production was characterized as development that fulfilled current requirements of individuals without compromising the requirements of individuals in the future (De Soete, 2016). As business partners of

global firms continued to question whether their
supply chains and production facilities were
sustainable, as well as safe, companies developed
goals to become environmentally sustainable through
green initiatives, the reduction of waste, and reduction
of carbon emissions (De Soete, 2016). To document
the organization's sustainability efforts, companies
worked with ERP providers to modify business
applications to create modules to track key
performance indicators (KPIs) and metrics. Zvezdov
and Hack (2016) performed a study of a multi-national
food company that created a carbon information
management (CIM) module within their ERP system
to track carbon emissions across their portfolio of
manufacturing facilities. In addition to carbon
emissions tracking, De Soete (2016) provided
examples of how organizations could have utilized
existing business applications to make more
sustainable decisions, including:

- Utilizing a product's bill of materials to track
  plastics' and solvents' use
- Tracking time durations of a chemical-
  synthesis step

- Analyzing energy consumption of a production line

Although initial steps had been taken to develop S-ERP applications, with the failure rates of traditional ERP implementations ranging in the area of 60% (Maas et al., 2014; Ravasan & Mansouri, 2016), the adoption of S-ERP applications could be complex to implement (Chofreh et al., 2016). Chofreh et al. (2016) posited the implementation of S-ERP applications introduce new territory for firms with new data types, data, and stakeholders – including environmentalists and scientists – that previously would not have interacted within an ERP application.

Traditional ERP applications were built upon optimizing operational and financial processes, which resulted in increased profits. In an S-ERP world, facets of TBL were implemented within an organization, which in turn affected the stakeholders (Chofreh et al., 2014). In comparing the two applications (ERP and S-ERP), traditional ERP systems focused primarily on profit to centralize data and decision-making functions within one application. Sustainable Enterprise Resource Planning's (S-ERP)

primary focus was on the Triple Bottom Line (TBL),
which was composed of profit, people, and planet
(Ahmad & Mehmood, 2015; Gianni, Gotzamani, &
Tsiotras, 2017). Profit within the TBL referred to
value-added activities performed within an
organization (Chofreh et al., 2014). The people
component referred to a firm's most important asset –
the employees. Planet refers to the environment and
the world's natural resources (Chofreh et al., 2016).
Although the environmental impact had not yet been
realized with a phased sustainability approach,
organizations could have leveraged technology to
have provided a positive impact on social change.

Implementing S-ERP Applications

As Information Technology (IT) projects had
varying methodologies, S-ERP applications could
have been implemented utilizing similar approaches
(Chofreh et al., 2016). Referring to the proposed S-
ERP implementation methodology as the S-ERP
master plan, this plan would have shortened the
implementation timeline, cost, and resources (Chofreh
et al., 2016). In developing a structured approach,

risk could have been mitigated throughout an implementation lifecycle. Similar to other implementation methodologies, the S-ERP methodology had three parts – the project roadmap, the application framework, and the project guidelines. In reviewing recent studies, a gap was identified regarding the outcome of successful S-ERP implementations. In reviewing the proposed architecture of an S-ERP application, Figure 3 depicted its complexity. Decision-makers in firms could have utilized existing technology, tools, and information they had at their disposal. Caveats could be identified during the implementation of S-ERP applications:

- Data management in organizations
- Data penetrations through ERP systems consistency in data logging
- Supply chain transparency
- Supply chain reliability
- The language (and education) issue (De Soete, 2016)

Leaders of organizations spoke to supply-chain concepts from a theoretical perspective and could have moved toward advanced, sustainable technologies to put business-related theories into practice.

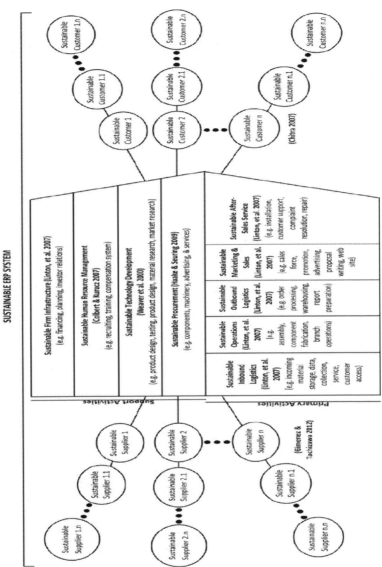

Figure 3 - Proposed S-ERP system with modules.
Adapted from "Sustainable Enterprise Resource Planning: Imperatives and Research Directions" by A. G. Chofreh, F. A. Goni, A. M. Shaharoun, S. Ismail, and J. J. Klemeš, 2014, Journal of Cleaner Production, 71, p. 141. Copyright 2014 by Elsevier Limited.

Enterprise Resource Planning Systems in Small- and Medium-sized Manufacturing Environments

Although ERP systems were initially developed to run large-scale enterprises, SMEs were motivated to introduce ERP implementations (Upadhyay, Basu, Adhikary, & Dan, 2010). Small- and medium-sized manufacturing enterprises were represented by a range of inherent characteristics that distinguished them from large enterprises, such as ownership type, structure, culture, and market (Amba & Abdulla, 2014). Researchers found ERP implementation costs, as a percent of revenue, ranged from 0.82% for large firms compared to 13.65% for SME firms, due to the economies of scale present in the larger firms (Bohórquez & Esteves, 2008).

Major projects planned for small- to medium-sized firms faced increased external and internal risks when compared to large organizations. Externally, small- to medium-sized enterprises were more fragile than large companies regarding sustainability and faced greater difficulty in obtaining credit (Zach & Munkvold, 2012). External risks such as the economy or increased customer demands could lead small- to medium-sized enterprises to delay the project of ERP implementation or forego it altogether. Internally, SMEs may find it difficult to implement re-engineering projects because of the small business' limited budget, manpower, or production resources. Small- to medium-sized enterprises may face greater challenges in adopting technology as compared to large enterprises, given the constraints mentioned (Zach & Munkvold, 2012).

Subject matter expert consultants should understand the total cost of ownership of an ERP application before embarking on a project of this magnitude given the hidden costs of ERP implementations. Successfully implemented, ERP applications allowed an organization to gain a competitive advantage by saving future resources and by enabling the company to respond to an ever-changing business environment (Mahdavian et al., 2016; Sudhaman & Thangavel, 2015). A successfully deployed ERP system could have increased customer satisfaction, reduced inefficient spending, strengthened sales and forecasts, reduced inventory turn-around times, and enhanced employee productivity (Maas et al., 2014). Because large enterprises had been implementing ERP solutions since the mid-1990s, SMEs viewed an ERP solution as 'the answer' to set the business apart from the competition. This opinion could be due to the SMEs lack of experience and in-depth knowledge of ERP implementations. If leaders of small- to medium-sized enterprises continued to implement these applications without training and education that instilled a true understanding of implementations and systems, and unless the differences between small- to medium-sized enterprises and large enterprises were clearly conceived, ERP implementations by consultants may continue to be painful and unfruitful (Huin, 2004).

Managerial Theories in ERP Implementations

Although researchers outlined various CFFs in the literature, management and leadership approaches and priorities were identified as failure factors in ERP implementations (Elkhani et al., 2014; Mitra & Mishra, 2016). Prior research focused on IT-related theories such as the task-technology-fit (TTF) theory and the Diffusion of Innovation (DOI) theory

(Pishdad et al., 2014). Researchers still identified a gap between leadership theories and ERP implementation risks.

Transformational leadership theory. Leaders were instruments of transformation exerted through the followers or employees to bring about change in governance and productivity (Dunn, Lafferty, & Alford, 2012; García-Morales, Jiménez-Barrionuevo, & Gutiérrez-Gutiérrez, 2012). First introduced by Burns (1978), transformational leadership was characterized as the ability of a leader to inspire employees to perform work beyond expectations (Elkhani et al., 2014). When leaders of organizations embarked on an ERP implementation, they performed an internal, business process re-engineering (BPR) initiative. With this new project, firms appointed a leader of the project that was equipped with BPR skills and with experience as a change agent (Mitra & Mishra, 2016).

In researching change management during ERP implementations, Iveroth (2016) found change management should have been at the top of executive's strategic agenda and leaders should have deferred to the empirical experience of internal and

external resources. Leaders should have been
transformational managers and focused on
continuous improvement, even after the project was
completed (Iveroth, 2016). Although external
consultants coordinating with the business leaders
likely had these skills, an internal change agent
included on the implementation team would have
influenced operational decisions.

Transformational leaders inspired, encouraged,
empowered, and influenced project team members to
work toward the common objective of a successful
implementation. When leaders encouraged creativity
through transformational leadership, users were more
likely to experiment with system features, enabling
workforce users to learn the system quicker (Elkhani
et al., 2014). Transformational leadership created a
higher level of psychological empowerment (PE),
commitment to the project, and trust (Mittal, 2016).

Leadership and organizational change helped
develop leaders and managers to adapt to change
and complex situations. Valuable information for
future leaders involved continued training in
specialized areas such communication, adapting to
change, complex situations, and effective leadership

and management skills. Research showed 65% of business leaders lacked global leadership skills, and less than 10% of organizations had a program in place to fill this skill and experience gap (Minner, 2015). There was room for management improvement achieved through transformational leadership.

Servant leadership theory. Another leadership theory compared to transformational leadership was servant leadership. In comparing the two theories, transformational leaders focused on organizational objectives while servant leaders focused on people as followers (Elkhani et al., 2014). Introduced by Greenleaf (1970, 1977), servant leadership included ethics, virtues, and morality and was noted as a model that assisted a leader in dealing with organizational issues. The primary objective of a servant leader was to empower followers to make a positive impact on the organization (Flynn, Smither, & Walker, 2015). Servant leaders were more empathetic than transformational leaders and incorporated emotional intelligence (EI). Kennedy (2012) found EI had more importance to multi-cultural leadership than task-related knowledge or IQ. An EI leader demonstrated the ability to identify not only the emotions of others, but also acknowledged personal bias. Emotional intelligence leadership became the base for servant leadership by promoting the others' strengths. In researching servant leadership qualities within ERP implementations, Krog and Govender (2015a) described five additional servant leadership dimensions: altruistic calling, emotional healing, wisdom, persuasive mapping, and organizational stewardship. Studies revealed persuasive mapping and altruistic caring led to employee empowerment, which in turn would have harnessed innovative behavior, commitment, and trust within ERP projects (Hassan, Asad, & Hoshino, 2016; Krog & Govender, 2015b). Little research had been performed (identified) on servant leadership related to the implementation of ERP applications, this research study focused on promoting the input of the stakeholders that participated in ERP projects.

Challenging Conventional Leadership

Although leaders in various industries had shifted to transformational or servant leadership, leaders of small- and medium-sized manufacturing organizations continued to follow conventional leadership methods (Larteb, Benhadou, Haddout, & Nahla, 2016; Ndalila, Mjema, Kundi, & Kerefu, 2015). To harness creativity and innovation to create a competitive advantage for an organization, leaders needed to transition from conventional leadership (Chawla & Sujatha, 2015). In the next section, approaches of how leaders have challenged conventional leadership will be reviewed (Acar, 2012).

Challenging conventional leadership with shared leadership. In the complex environment of increased global presence, conventional wisdoms and old managerial approaches were continually challenged. Leaders needed to be improvisational and innovative as organizations leveraged technology to gain a competitive edge over their competitors (Kasemsap, 2016; Ranjan, Jha, & Pal, 2016). To

expand on this philosophy, former General Electric,
Chief Executive Officer, Jack Welch posited, "if the
outside environment is changing faster than the inside
environment, the company is doomed" (Harvey &
Buckley, 2002, p. 371). Although there may not have
been a universal managerial approach, managers
analyzed their current business environment,
reflected on the organization's strategic vision, and
acted on complexities that business organizations
faced in the late 2010s.

Mitra and Mishra (2016) stated leadership was
the most important factor in a successful (or
unsuccessful) ERP implementation. Given ERP
applications integrated operational and financial
functions of an organization, traditional hierarchical
leadership approaches proved unfavorable in these
projects. With the cross-functional engagement
requirements, a distribution of leadership was
required. The concept of shared leadership was a
concept studied at the executive and board member
level. To place shared leadership at the ERP project
level, this approach improved team effectiveness by
sharing responsibilities, resulting in collaboration,
trust, and mutual accountability (Le Pennec &

Raufflet, 2016). Given younger professionals were more technologically experienced, and more tenured professionals had years of managerial experience, a shared leadership approach could have been executed during ERP implementations. In this approach, blending technical and managerial experience led to successful ERP implementations within business organizations.

Challenging conventional leadership with sponsor-leader exchange. Because ERP projects lasted from six months to two years (Bansal & Agarwal, 2015), power struggles arose among project leaders and team members. In the world of ERP implementations, a common misconception was when one referred to a leader within a project, they were referring to upper-level management. The leader could have been an internal project manager, an external project manager or lead consultant, and organizational leaders were referred to as executive sponsors. Firms of all sizes implemented enterprise applications, and leaders from different departments were identified as the project leader, resulting in various leadership styles. One managerial approach extensively researched in the area of leadership was the leader-manager exchange (LMX). Leaders performed knowledge-sharing to provide the agreed-upon vision of the firm's leadership team. A leader-manager exchange led to employee commitment and job satisfaction within an organization (Hall, Baker, Andrews, Hunt, & Rapp, 2015).

In translating this approach to ERP projects, when the executive sponsor (corporate leader) assigned a project leader to the implementation, that assigned leader must outline organizational reasons to embark on implementing a new business application in a concept coined as sponsor-leader exchange (SLX). By instituting an SLX approach in an ERP implementation, the leader not only shared information with managers and employees, but also shared tasks and responsibilities. This approach enabled alignment throughout the organization's network, but also increased interpersonal trust between centralized leadership, decentralized management, and the employees of the organization (Scandura & Pellegrini, 2008). In the implementation of SLX, project team members had the ability to take the information regarding the executive sponsor's vision and knowledge of the application to other organizational employees, enabling empowerment, decentralized decision-making, and job enrichment.

In reflecting on transformational and servant leadership theories, one possible conclusion was the appropriate approach was dependent on the project and culture of the organization. To enhance the innovativeness and creativity within ERP implementations, firms implemented a blended transformational and servant leadership approach (Elkhani et al., 2014). Challenging conventional leadership, shared leadership and SLX shared responsibilities of implementation to harness the experiences and creativity of all project members. While there was no one-size-fits-all approach, as the business landscape changed, firms looked for innovative ways to mitigate risk, while at the same time remaining sustainable within respective business markets.

Benefits of ERP Systems

As the global market shrank as technological and logistical advances increased, leadership teams of organizations looked for ways to make strategic decisions to maintain or increase market share in respective industries. To turn these systems into a competitive advantage, leaders of firms utilized ERP systems to make operational, tactical, and strategic processes increasingly efficient and effective (Shao et al., 2015). Enterprise Resource Planning systems were customized, integrated, and packaged as software-based systems that handled system requirements in functional areas of a business, including: finance, human resources, manufacturing, sales and marketing (Lin, 2010). In addition to using ERP systems as a tool to make daily business decisions, these systems were used as a tool to improve knowledge sharing within the organization. ERP applications enabled departments and facilities to share knowledge and collaborate instead of operating within disparate systems.

Technological benefits of ERP systems. Enterprise Resource Planning systems made internal advances by shrinking the supply chain for organizations' networks and brought competitive advantages to enterprises. The advances included a reduction of business costs, quick response to customers, and acceleration of corporate connections (Tsai et al., 2011). Enterprise Resource Planning systems increased an organization's financial performance by reduction of turnover for inventory, increased turnover for receivables, and increased profit margins.

Enterprise Resource Planning systems impacted social change by passing on cost savings, as well as communicating important information generated by these systems, to the consumer. In studies, researchers found ERP systems increased trading partner satisfaction with the use of the Supplier Relationship Management (SMR) and Customer Relationship Management (CRM) modules and applications. In one study, May, Dhillon, and Caldeira (2013) found ERP systems ensured the ability for firms to understand customer desires by providing suggestions based on buying patterns generated by the application. Amazon uses this type of application, generating related and relatable product-buying suggestions once a targeted product is reviewed or purchased by the consumer. With increased communication and visibility via the ERP system(s), organizations worked closer with business partners to build stronger commercial alliances.

Knowledge sharing benefits of ERP

systems. Knowledge sharing could be included with

the implementation of ERP-based applications, given

that ERP systems could be leveraged to positively

impact management decisions. Knowledge sharing,

also known as knowledge transfer, was defined as the

process through which one organizational unit was

affected by the experience of another. The first entity

learned from an event and, in turn, the second entity

learns from the experience of the first, e.g.,

cooperative learning (Rezania & Ouedraogo, 2013).

When organizations implemented ERP systems, they

hired outside consultants with knowledge of the

application and familiarity of industry best-practices

needed to successfully implement these ERP

applications and solutions. Although selecting an

experienced consultant was a critical success factor

in implementation and maintenance of an ERP

system (Maditinos et al., 2012), the effective transfer

of knowledge was more vital. Jeng and Dunk (2013)

found knowledge creation within a firm was a stronger

predictor of ERP implementation success. As

organizational leaders continued to build a knowledge base throughout the ERP implementation lifecycle, the knowledge base also increased the likelihood of a successful ERP installation.

Regarding social impact, companies are using technology to alert vendors and customers of inventory levels and forecasts resulting in better management of supply chains. Real-time inventory data benefited organizations and enabled management to make timely decisions on production spikes, manpower and labor scheduling, as well as transportation and logistics planning to meet the consumer needs for products or services during seasonal or marketing-result demands.

While technology and knowledge sharing impacted positive social change within an organization, management and leadership also played an important role.

Leadership benefits of ERP systems. When organizational leaders made the decision to bring new technology within an organization, management teams played a key role in the decision-making process throughout the life of an ERP implementation.

For a new technology installation to be successful,
management buy-in was one of the critical success
factors. Researchers found top executive
management support was a prerequisite for a
successful ERP system implementation (Maditinos et
al., 2012). Lin (2010) concluded top executive
management support influenced both perceived
usefulness and ERP system usage by the workforce –
after the implementation. With the level of change of
an ERP implementation, some leaders may have
encountered resistance from their workforce, which
indicated a need for leadership opinions and
viewpoint changes.

Once an ERP application was installed,
management support should not stop. The
organizations' management team must practice
continuous improvement methods to realize the full
capability of the implemented ERP applications within
any operational process or procedure. In
organizations that installed ERP systems, the post-
implementation called for intensive interactions
among managers and system users to share
knowledge creation, extraction, preservation, and
learning (Tsai et al., 2011). Re-written policies,

procedures, how-to manuals enabled best-practices in the use of the new system. Throughout the life of the installed ERP-based application, management must periodically review the usage of the ERP application to ensure users were not reverting to legacy systems and external applications. Otherwise, reverting created islands of information and discordance in work processes and procedures. From a strategic management perspective, Maditinos et al. (2012) found when top management worked closely with ERP users, the communication between business groups was enhanced and conflict resolution was attainable. Based on a review of the academic research on technology and knowledge sharing in organizations related to ERP implementations, stakeholders of an organization should be held accountable for the long-term success of the installed ERP application.

Common Methods and Techniques Used to Research ERP Implementations

Research methods and techniques conducted on ERP implementations in small- and medium-sized manufacturing environments were analyzed for this research study. Quantitative, qualitative, and mixed methods studies were conducted on critical success factors in ERP implementations, with researchers outlining the strengths and weaknesses of each method. Several approaches and techniques were identified for each design, but the most cited approaches were targeted for discussion.

Quantitative studies were used in analyzing critical success factors in ERP implementations because quantitative research designs were more amenable to the topic than qualitative designs (Hicks & Berg, 2014). Quantitative studies ranged from causal-comparative designs (Bansal & Agarwal, 2015; Ravasan & Mansouri, 2016; Uwizeyemungu & Raymond, 2009) to correlational designs (Beheshti et al., 2014; Garg & Agarwal, 2014; Ram & Corkindale, 2014). Surveys were the most referenced quantitative approach in reviewing critical success factors in small- and medium-sized manufacturing ERP implementations (Ab Talib & Abdul Hamid, 2014; Ab Talib, Abdul Hamid, & Thoo, 2015; Bansal & Agarwal, 2015; Pishdad et al., 2014). Surveys were used to quantify current and future states of ERP

implementations in small- and medium-sized
manufacturing environments (Tatari, Castro-
Lacouture, & Skibniewski, 2007). In surveys, the
Likert-type scale was the most used scale for
measuring patterns, attitudes, and opinions of
participants responding to critical success factors in
ERP implementations (Costa, Ferreira, Bento, &
Aparicio, 2016; Garg & Agarwal, 2014; Tatari et al.,
2007).

In research conclusions to identifying critical
success factors, Gajic et al. (2014) stated quantitative
studies on ERP applications and their impact on
business performance were not sufficient. Markus,
Axline, Petrie, and Tanis (2000) concluded the
economic benefits of ERP applications were difficult
to measure through the use of quantitative analysis.
Researchers who analyzed critical success factors in
ERP implementations used qualitative case studies
(Abdelmoniem, 2016; Alharthi et al., 2017; Mo & He,
2015; Saade & Nijher, 2016) and phenomenological
research designs (Jrad & Sundaram, 2015; Yurtseven
& Buchanan, 2016).

During the review of the literature, the mixed
method approach was cited less often than

quantitative and qualitative methods. Mixed methods may have been effective when one research method could have been used to inform as a basis or reference to the other (Fetters, Curry, & Creswell, 2013). In research studies on ERP critical success factors, where either the qualitative or quantitative data were lacking, a mixed method approach assisted in strengthening the study (Gajic et al., 2014). In the ERP implementation studies that included both interviews and surveys, researchers deferred to a mixed method design to conduct research (Dwivedi et al., 2015; Peng & Nunes, 2013). The mixed-methods approach provided an in-depth, contextualized, insight of qualitative data, research coupled with more efficient, but less-rich, quantitative research (Zha & Tu, 2016), resulted in an disadvantage in that mixed-methods research was more time-consuming compared to other methods.

Ali and Miller (2017) concluded because the findings in ERP studies were repetitive and lacked empirical research, scholars and practitioners should collaborate to produce more innovative research techniques. Scholtz, Calitz, and Cilliers (2013) found empirical studies on small- and medium-sized enterprises were limited. Aligned with this research study, Scholtz et al. (2013) outlined the importance of consultants to identify critical success factors in an ERP implementation. By developing a sample size of experienced consultants, a larger sample size of ERP implementations was measured in this research study, as subject matter expert consultants had already implemented multiple ERP applications during their career. Because these consultants had performed multiple ERP implementations, using a Delphi approach, each CSF was measured to establish a more defined list of CSFs that SMEs could have been used to implement future ERP solutions.

Gaps in the Literature

A review of the literature recognized that ERP implementations continued to fail for identified reasons. Although researchers had concluded top management support, user feedback, training and education, project management, and ERP package selection were factors that could have mitigated the risk of failed implementations, a gap in the academic literature still existed (Baykasoğlu & Gölcük, 2017;

Leyh & Sander, 2015; Shao, Feng, & Hu, 2016; Sun
et al., 2015; Tarhini et al., 2015). The goal of this
research study was to narrow the scholar-practitioner
gap, given the lack of consensus regarding critical
success factors identified in the literature versus
those applied in small- and medium-sized
manufacturing environments.

In performing a literature search on positive
social change and ERP implementations, the search
results uncovered the gap still existed on the topic
(Elbardan & Kholeif, 2017; Seth et al., 2017).
Narrowing this gap contributed to positive social
change by working toward building a consensus
among ERP manufacturing consultants and scholars
to improve project success and the triple bottom line
for large enterprises and small- and medium-sized
enterprises in the manufacturing industry. By
producing the results and following the conclusions of
this research study, the scholar-practitioner gap was
narrowed by reviewing and implementing the
identified top critical success factors.

Chapter 3

Research Method

The purpose of this qualitative modified Delphi study was to identify a consensus among a panel of ERP manufacturing consultants as to the desirability and feasibility of critical success factors in ERP implementations in the United States. The study involved sampling an expert panel of ERP manufacturing consultants, who participated in three rounds of online surveys. Data collection continued until consensus was identified in Round 3.

Enterprise projects were complex, and required resources, time, and were capital intensive (Bansal & Agarwal, 2015). Although these applications could have led to a strategic competitive advantage for an organization (Habibzadeh et al., 2016), failed implementations required additional research on

critical success factors in IS projects (Schönberger &
Čirjevskis, 2017). Due to increased competitiveness
and customer expectations within the small- and
medium-sized manufacturing sector, ERP
implementation critical success factors were
suggested to be periodically reviewed for refinement
(Rashid et al., 2018; Sharma et al., 2015). The critical
success factors noted in the literature review may no
longer apply (Saade & Nijher, 2016). This research
study uncovered critical success factors previously
unexplored through the narrative comments from the
panelists in Round 1.

Research Design and Rationale

The research in this study was undertaken to
identify a consensus among a panel of ERP
manufacturing consultants as to the desirability and
feasibility of critical success factors in ERP
implementations in the United States. The research
question and sub-questions were:

RQ1: What is the level of consensus among ERP manufacturing consultants as to the desirability and feasibility of critical success factors for ERP implementations?

RQ1 Sub-question 1: What is the level of consensus among ERP manufacturing consultants as to the desirability of critical success factors for ERP implementations?

RQ1 Sub-question 2: What is the level of consensus among ERP manufacturing consultants as to the feasibility of critical success factors for ERP implementations?

A review of research methods conducted on ERP implementations in small- and medium-sized manufacturing environments was analyzed (Ngai et al., 2008; Remus & Wiener, 2010; Zeng et al., 2015). After appraising quantitative, qualitative, and mixed methods research designs, the qualitative method was selected for further qualitative research on ERP implementations in small- and medium-sized manufacturing enterprises (Ho & Lin, 2004; Ngai et al., 2004; Scholtz et al., 2013). The qualitative method was chosen to identify patterns among critical success factors in ERP implementations (Pishdad et al., 2014; Ravasan & Mansouri, 2016; Shen et al., 2016; Turner, 2014).

To answer the research questions, qualitative approaches were reviewed, including: grounded theory, phenomenology, and the Delphi method. Although grounded theory was a valuable approach when collecting empirical research (Eisenhardt, 1989; Orlikowski, 1993), this approach was not selected. The aim of the study was not to explain ERP implementations by developing a theory grounded in the data (Glaser & Strauss, 2012). The goal of this study was to establish a consensus to the desirability and feasibility of critical success factor benchmarks for ERP implementations. A phenomenological approach was not chosen given its focus on exploring the essence and meaning participants attach to the lived experience of a particular phenomenon (Moustakas, 1994). The Delphi method was selected for this study given its record as a best-practice approach to identifying long-term trends in technology (Adler & Ziglio, 1996; Linstone & Turoff, 2002).

The Delphi technique was a qualitative
research design used to establish a consensus
through the input from a panel of experts without the
requirement of face-to-face interactions (Linstone &
Turoff, 2002; von der Gracht & Darkow, 2013). A
classical Delphi technique consisted of three rounds
of surveys to reach a consensus. The typical panel
size in a classical Delphi study consisted of six to 12
experts (Habibi et al., 2014; Romano, 2010). Round
1 of a classical Delphi is typically composed of open-
ended questions to explore the research topic fully
(Adler & Ziglio, 1996; Linstone & Turoff, 2002;
Skulmoski, Hartman, & Krahn, 2010).

A modified approach was an iterative data
collection procedure that relied on a panel of experts
to analyze the future state of a scenario or
phenomena (Elnasr et al., 2012; Hsu & Sandford,
2007). Modified Delphi studies were based on what
was already known about a topic (as available in the
literature) (Keeney, Hasson, & McKenna, 2006; Upton
& Upton, 2006). Because Round 1 of this study was
composed of closed-ended questions rated on a scale
and the expert panel proposed modifications to
existing critical success factors, the approach was

identified as a modified Delphi study. A modified
Delphi approach was conducted because the Delphi
study was composed of a targeted sample of 42 ERP
manufacturing consultants with the research goal to
narrow a gap in the research (Hung et al., 2016; Zeng
et al., 2015).

In Delphi studies focused on ERP
implementations, researchers indicated future
research should be conducted using larger sample
sizes, as the results may be more useful given
smaller Delphi groups faced with potential bias
(Chuang, Lin, Chen, Chen, & Wang, 2015).
Compared to other Delphi studies conducted on a
small subset of ERP manufacturing consultants to
analyze critical success factors (Bansal & Agarwal,
2015; Islam, Anis, & Abdullah, 2015; Sun et al.,
2015), finding a consensus among ERP consultants
provided a more holistic view of critical success
factors for manufacturers regardless of the chosen
solution, because of the panelists' diverse
perspectives. Hiring consultants was a common
practice for organizations implementing ERP solutions
(Chang et al., 2013; Mitra & Mishra, 2016). In this
research study's findings, the researcher's goal was

to provide a forward-looking analysis on critical success factors, scholars, practitioners, and firms for implementation and practice as the manufacturing industry moved further into Industry 4.0.

Role of the Researcher

The researcher was the primary source of instrumentation, data collection, and analysis for this study. The researcher drew from professional networks through LinkedIn groups to recruit SME panelists. Professional relationships may have existed between the researcher and the study participants, who remained anonymous. The researcher did not have supervisory or instructor relationships with any of the participants. Although a member of the LinkedIn groups in which the researcher asked permission to post the survey, to reduce researcher bias, the researcher joined other groups to reduce the likelihood of having relationships with study participants within the LinkedIn groups.

To mitigate the risk of bias due to the researcher's ERP manufacturing consulting experience, the approach of Polkinghorne (1989) was used to support the validity of the findings. The first

phase of the Delphi study was qualitative in nature,
Polkinghorne's (1989), so the five questions
established provided a foundation for validation in the
study:

- Did the researcher influence the participants'
  descriptions that do not reflect their empirical
  experience?
- Were the survey questions easily understood?
- In analyzing the surveys, were there other
  conclusions that could have been derived? If
  so, where these identified?
- Was it possible to disseminate the responses
  and relate to the panelists' experience?
- Was the survey description situation specific?

After performing the narrative data collection,
the researcher analyzed the data through Likert-type
responses using coding and statistical means. The
Likert-type scale was used to provide accurate
information about the panelists' perceptions to answer
the research questions (Oppenheim, 1992). This
approach led to more valid and reliable research
because the data were collected through online

surveys, which increased its diversity while reducing chances of error and bias. When data were collected through these methods, there were fewer chances the information gathered could potentially contain bias (Burkholder, Cox, & Crawford, 2016). The resulting research was more accurate, and the data analysis techniques reduced bias.

Methodology

Research questions drove the research methodology used (Coyle & Tickoo, 2007; Creswell, 2007, 2009). The research methodology provided the foundation for a study, as well as the framework for participant selection, data collection methods and processes, and data analysis (Burkholder et al., 2016; Frankfort-Nachmias & Nachmias, 2009). Qualitative studies reviewed included a range of approaches. After performing an analysis, the researcher focused on the qualitative Delphi method. The Delphi method was used to anticipate long-term trends in technology (Adler & Ziglio, 1996; Linstone & Turoff, 2002). The researcher used this method to rely on the subject matter experts' opinions to predict outcomes of critical

success factors in ERP implementations within small-
and medium -sized manufacturing environments.

Target Population

The target population for this study were
manufacturing consultants in the United States with
experience in ERP implementations. Enterprise
Resource Planning manufacturing consultant SMEs
were regarded as the experts in their specified
manufacturing sector and were trained in technical
and practical implementations of enterprise
applications (Chang et al., 2013; Mitra & Mishra,
2016). These consultants spent a large amount of
time at customer sites during implementations, so
were typically distributed across the United States to
support their clients' facilities and projects.
Determining the number of consultants in the target
population in the United States that supported ERP
implementations was difficult due to an increasing
number of small- and medium-sized manufacturing
organizations implementing ERP applications (Mayeh,
Ramayah, & Mishra, 2016; Soler, Feliks, &
Ömürgönülşen, 2016). The U.S. government

estimated the number of consultants nationwide had grown to 993,000 by 2020; therefore, an estimate of approximately 200,000 consultants would be included in the ERP application industry segment (Joshi, Kuhn, & Niederman, 2010; Orr & Orr, 2013). Although the current study could have included ERP project managers as the expert panel to expedite the rate of reply, choosing ERP consultants provided a ground-level view of critical success factors identified in ERP implementations.

The participants for this study were selected based on ERP implementation experience, not their location relative to geographical region. The researcher solicited participants for this study through the following 10 groups on LinkedIn: (a) SAP Community; (b) Dynamics AX ERP Professionals Group; (c) Oracle ERP User Network; (d) JD Edwards OneWorld and EnterpriseOne Professionals; (e) Microsoft Dynamics 365; (f) QAD Community; (g) Infor Global Solutions Professionals; (h) Netsuite Users Group; (i) Epicor ERP 10 Consultants; and, (j) Acumatica ERP Software User Group. These LinkedIn groups focused on connecting ERP consultants to share knowledge and best practices devoted to specific applications knowledge and ranged from between 175 to 342,000 members.

See Appendix A for the request sent to each LinkedIn group moderator to post the study invitation to their group. The invitation message appears in Appendix B. To reduce researcher bias, the researcher joined other LinkedIn groups from which participants were solicited to reduce the likelihood of having (social media) relationships with study participants prior to submission of the request for approval for the study to the Institutional Review Board (IRB). The selection of ERP manufacturing experts that implemented different ERP solutions produced unbiased results due to varied implementation methodologies, application functionalities, and organizational cultures.

Participant Selection Logic

The selection of participants was the cornerstone to a successful Delphi study and enabled the ability to obtain valid and trustworthy results (Lohuis, van Vuuren, & Bohlmeijer, 2013; Orte, Ballester, Amer, & Vives, 2014; Steurer, 2011).

Because consultants may not have possessed in-depth knowledge of some of the critical success factors identified in the survey, an uneven distribution of experience may have been represented in the research results (Hsu & Sandford, 2007). To minimize an uneven distribution, the study involved a purposive sampling technique to ensure meaningful results in the study. The purposive sampling technique, also known as judgment sampling, was a non-probability approach identified as most effective when a study required expert knowledge within a domain (Etikan, Musa, & Alkassim, 2016). In purposive sampling, the aim was to reach data saturation (Guest, Bunce, & Johnson, 2006; Ravitch & Carl, 2016). Purposive sampling was appropriate to this research study given the purpose of the Delphi technique was to obtain expert opinions from the SME participants (Fink & Kosecoff, 1985).

To acquire the relevant research data, the researcher targeted ERP manufacturing consultants as the expert panel for this study. Participants for the study were selected based on the following criteria: (a) at least five years of experience implementing ERP applications; (b) had performed ERP implementations in the United States; (c) had performed ERP implementations in the industrial or manufacturing sector; and, (d) had performed ERP implementations for small- and medium-sized enterprises (firms that employed fewer than 500 employees). The ERP manufacturing consultants self-selected based on the criteria provided in the researcher's invitation to participate. After completing the informed consent, the participants were presented with screening questions and prompted to check yes or no in response to the questions (see Appendix C). If they selected no for any of the questions, they were thanked for their interest and unable to access the survey.

The minimum recommended response rate for each round is between 40% and 50% (Atkinson & Gold, 2001). At least 125 consultants were solicited in Round 1 of this study and targeted to achieve saturation in the narrative data, as well as to retain the target sample size of a minimum of 50 ERP manufacturing consultants for subsequent and final rounds of data collection. Data saturation in qualitative research occurred when new themes were no longer found, and enough data had been collected

to replicate the study (Fusch & Ness, 2015; Ravitch &
Carl, 2016). Although Delphi studies typically ranged
between 15 to 20 participants (Hsu & Sandford,
2007), at least 125 consultants were solicited in
Round 1 of this study to achieve saturation in the
narrative data and to retain the Round 3 target
sample size for the subsequent rounds of data
collection. The exact number was difficult to
determine due to the solicitation process via the social
media platform.

Because of the length of the study and the
multiple rounds of data collection, the goal was to
alleviate the possibility of participants dropping out
during multiple points of the study. To alleviate this
risk, the researcher outlined the premise of a Delphi
study in the survey invitation, stated there would be a
minimum of three rounds, and noted this research
study would build on the knowledge of the ERP
consulting practice.

Instrumentation

In the literature review research on critical
success factors, Sun et al. (2015) identified more than

80 critical success factors. The Round 1 instrument in this research study was limited to critical success factors identified by Saade and Nijher (2016). In their study, Saade and Nijher performed a literature review of 37 case studies from different countries and contexts. The results of their study resulted in a consolidated list of 22 distinct critical success factors that applied to the five ERP implementation stages identified by Saade and Nijher, including: (a) the organizational state, (b) business requirements gathering, (c) the proposed technical solution, (d) implementation, and (e) post-implementation.

The data collection instruments in this study consisted of online surveys. These surveys were administered through SurveyMonkey, a secure online survey provider platform. In the first round, the expert panel of ERP manufacturing consultants were asked to complete the survey outlined in Appendix D. The expert panel rated critical success factors on a 5-point Likert-type scale. The Likert-scale ranged from 1 to 5 where the ratings were: 1-highly undesirable, 2-undesirable, 3-neutral, 4-desirable, and 5-highly desirable. Using the definitions outlined by Linstone and Turoff (2002), the following desirability

descriptions were included to provide clarity for the
participants: 1-highly undesirable: had a major
negative impact to the implementation; 2-undesirable:
had a negative impact to the implementation with little
positive to no positive effect; 3-neutral: had no impact
on the implementation; 4-desirable: had a minimal
positive impact to the implementation with little
negative effect; and 5-highly desirable: had a positive
impact to the implementation with no negative effect.

In addition to the instrument outlined above,
the Round 1 survey included demographic questions.
The demographic questions included (a) age range,
(b) gender, (c) education level, (d) years of
experience, (e) number of implementations completed
in small- and medium-sized manufacturing
environments (organizations that employ less than
500 employees), and (f) geographic region.
Identifying the demographic characteristics of the
study participants validated the level of distribution
among the expert panel regarding their expertise and
experience. The age range choices on the survey
were: (a) 21 and under, (b) 22 to 34, (c) 35 to 44, (d)
45 to 54, (e) 55 to 64, and (f) 65 and over. The
participants entered gender in response to a question

in the survey. The choices for participants' years of experience were: (a) 5 to 10 years, (b) 11 to 15 years, (c) 16 to 20 years, and (d) 21 years or more. The choices for participants' highest education level were: (a) high school diploma, (b) bachelor's degree, (c) master's degree, and (d) doctoral degree. The choices for the number of implementations the participant completed in small- and medium-sized manufacturing environments were: (a) 1 to 5, (b) 6 to 10, (c) 11 to 15, (d) 16 to 20, and, (e) 20 or more. The choices for geographic regions were: (a) Northeast, (b) Midwest, (c) Southeast, (d) Southwest, and (e) West. The participants were also encouraged to add ERP factors not outlined in the survey. After reviewing the responses, the 10 critical success factors with the highest frequency were moved to Round 2 of the study.

In Round 2 the panelists rated the desirability and feasibility of the critical success factors using two separate 5-point Likert-type scales. The instrument included the 10 top critical success factors identified in Round 1. The ratings on the scale ranged from 1 to 5: 1-highly undesirable/highly infeasible, 2-undesirable /infeasible, 3-neutral, 4-desirable/feasible, and 5-highly desirable/highly feasible. In Round 2, participants were provided with the same descriptions for desirability as were used in Round 1.

The following feasibility descriptions were included to provide clarity for the participants including desirability descriptions (Ravasan & Mansouri, 2016; Linstone & Turoff, 2002): (a) highly infeasible: should not be implemented due to the project schedule, cost, or resource constraints; (b) infeasible: some indication or empirical experience the critical success factor should not be implemented due to an impact to the project schedule, cost, or resource constraints; (c) neutral: will have no impact on the implementation; (d) feasible: some indication or empirical experience this critical success factor can be implemented successfully without an impact to the project schedule, cost, or resources; and (e) highly feasible: this critical success factor can be implemented successfully without an impact to the project schedule, cost, or resources. The critical success factors with the highest ratings of desirability and feasibility in Round 2 were moved into Round 3, during which the ERP manufacturing consultants rated the remaining critical success factors for desirability and feasibility. The same desirability and feasibility descriptions used in Round 2 were presented to the participants in Round 3. Subsequent rounds of rating were not required as consensus was reached in Round 3.

Field Test

Prior to the IRB approval, the study included a field test of the Round 1 survey to test the clarity and relevance of the open-ended questions on the research survey. In Figure 4, the researcher outlined the critical success factors used in the field test to ensure the experts understood the scope of the research. San-Jose and Retolaza (2016) emphasized the phrasing of a survey ensured participants accurately answered the questions. The goal of the field test was to identify ambiguities in the objective, definitions, and survey questions. Data were not collected in the field test.

Cultural Change Readiness (CCR)	Detailed data migration plan (DMP)
Top Management Support and Commitment (TMSC)	Measurable Goals (MG)
Knowledge Capacity Production Network (KCPN)	Small Internal Team of Best Employees (STBE)
Minimum Customization (MC)	Open and Transparent Communication (OTC)
Legacy Systems Support (LSS)	Base Point Analysis (BPA)
ERP Fit with Organization (EFO)	Morale Maintenance (MM)
Local Vendors Partnership (LVP)	Contingency Plans (CP)
Detailed Cost (DC)	ERP Success Documentation (ESD)
Business Process Re-engineering (BPR)	User Feedback Usage (UFU)
Quality Management (QM)	Maximum Potential Usage (MPU)
Risk Management (RM)	Results Measurement (RM)

Figure 4 - ERP critical success factors.
Adapted from "Critical Success Factors in Enterprise Resource Planning implementation: A Review of Case Studies" by R. G. Saade and H. Nijher, 2016, Journal of Enterprise Information Management, 29, p. 88. Copyright 2016 by Emerald Group Publishing Limited.

In the field test, eight experts with knowledge of ERP implementations and item construction reviewed the surveys for face and content validity of the questions. Four of the eight experts who

participated in the field test had experience with ERP
implementations in an academic setting and four had
experience consulting within the ERP manufacturing
industry (connected with through LinkedIn). The
researcher messaged them the study instrument to
initiate a request for feedback. In conducting this
study's literature review, the researcher uncovered
four academic ERP experts who previously chaired
dissertations on the topics of ERP applications or
Delphi studies. Using their contact information, the
researcher sent an email explaining the purpose of
the field test and requested feedback. All surveys
were returned by the eight ERP experts within two
days of sending the surveys. The participants in the
survey instrument field test did not participate in the
main study.

The field test experts were emailed the Round
1 survey questions for feedback. After reviewing the
questions, the experts provided feedback on the
clarity and relevance of the questions by responding
to two questions about the survey (see Appendix E for
the field test questions). Based on the feedback, the
survey questions for Round 1 were modified. The
feedback from this field test assisted in identifying

areas revised before the main study commenced.

One of the experts stated they had to read the survey objective twice before understanding how to answer the survey questions. With this feedback, the researcher rephrased the objective to make it more understandable to the expert panel before Round 1 began. Regarding the definitions for the study, one of the experts stated they were somewhat unclear of the local vendor's partnership metrics. To resolve this issue, the researcher added additional definitions to this metric to ensure the modified Delphi research participants fully understood the critical success factor when taking the survey. The results of the field test are outlined in Chapter 4.

Internal Consistency Reliability

To test the internal reliability of each of the items pertaining to critical success factors in Round 2 and Round 3, Cronbach's (1951) coefficient alphas were calculated in SPSS using the main study data. Cronbach's alpha was used to examine the internal consistency reliability of multipoint scales (Heitner, Kahn, & Sherman, 2013; Tavakol & Dennick, 2011).

Ranging from 0 to 1, the closer the coefficient value was to 1, the more reliable the scale (Anderson & Gerbing, 1988). A value greater than or equal to 0.7 was an acceptable reliability coefficient (Nunnally, 1967; Wijkstra et al., 1994).

Procedures for Recruitment, Participation, and Data Collection

Procedures for recruitment. Permission was obtained from each LinkedIn group moderator to post the research survey to their respective LinkedIn groups. Using social media in conjunction with an online survey tool reduced the time to collect data, and also allowed access to a larger pool of ERP manufacturing consultants for the expert panel.

Procedures for participation. Participants were presented with an invitation post on their respective LinkedIn group pages that included information about the research purpose, as well as the SurveyMonkey link to access the URL for the informed consent process and the survey. The invitation post also included the researcher's contact information if participants had questions regarding the study. To minimize the time for the data collection, the researcher asked the participants to submit the survey within a set time period for each round of the research study.

Data collection. The study spanned 1.5 months due to the iterative nature of a Delphi study. Delphi studies can take circa 45 days to administer while allowing the ERP manufacturing consultants two weeks to respond during each study round (Delbecq, Gustafson, & Van de Ven, 1986; Ludwig, 1997).

The researcher's Delphi study involved three rounds of data collection and analysis. The survey data were collected through SurveyMonkey, a secure online survey platform. Online surveys were advantageous in studies where controlled samples are required (Burgess, Sellitto, Cox, & Buultjens, 2011; Evans & Mathur, 2005). Performing an online survey provided speed, convenience, and cost savings compared to conventional surveys (Dixon & Turner, 2007; Evans & Mathur, 2005). Figure 5 included the strengths and weaknesses of online surveys.

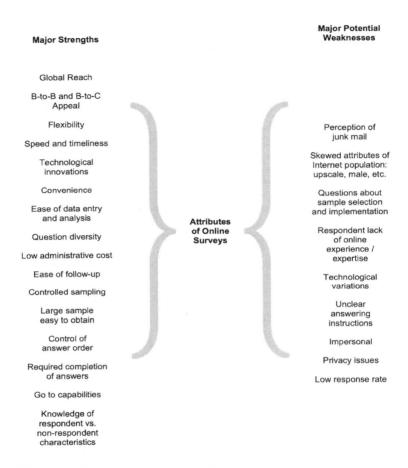

Figure 5 - Online survey strengths and weaknesses.
Adapted from "The Value of Online Surveys" by J. R. Evans
and A. Mathur, 2005, Internet Research, 15, p. 197. Copyright
2005 by Emerald Group Publishing.

In the first round, the expert panel of
consultants were asked to provide narrative
comments on the existing critical success factors.

The participants were also encouraged to provide additional factors not outlined in the survey. After reviewing the responses, the top 10 critical success factors with the highest desirability were moved to Round 2 of the study.

Round 2 data asked the ERP manufacturing consultants' ratings of the desirability and feasibility of the top 10 most desirable critical success factors from Round 1 using two separate 5-point Likert-type scales. The top two percentages (rating of 4 or 5) with 75% or higher on both desirability and feasibility scales were moved to Round 3. Because percentage agreement and median of agreement may be used in the same Delphi study (Heitner et al., 2013), the researcher also examined each critical success factor's median score. A median score of greater than or equal to 3.5 was identified as an acceptable consensus in a Delphi study (Diamond et al., 2014; Fox et al., 2016; Paoloni et al., 2017). Median scores of 3.5 or higher items were included in Round 3.

Round 3 data were comprised of the ERP manufacturing consultants' ratings of the remaining critical success factors for desirability and feasibility. In Delphi studies, consensus was reached when saturation of opinion occurs, or when sufficient is information exchanged (Skulmoski et al., 2010). To determine the level of consensus, researchers identified that when 75% of experts selected a 4 or 5 on a Likert-type scale, consensus was met (Diamond et al., 2014; Fox et al., 2016; Paoloni et al., 2017). Although the researcher used a median score in Round 2, only the top two percentages with 75% or higher on both desirability and feasibility scales were used for Round 3.

Although researchers noted Delphi studies required three or more rounds to reach a consensus (Hasson & Keeney, 2011; Loo, 2002; Powell, 2003), Taraba, Mikusz, and Herzwurm (2014) concluded the majority of changes occurred in the first two rounds of a Delphi study. According to Mitchell (1991), "there is not much gained in conventional Delphi by iterating more than twice" (p. 347). The current study participants were informed a maximum of five rounds would take place to reach a consensus, given the lack of consensus in literature regarding the appropriate (best practice) number of rounds. Subsequent rounds of rating were not required, as consensus was reached in Round 3.

After all responses were received, the
summary data from SurveyMonkey was downloaded
to a spreadsheet and the data were reviewed for
incomplete or inaccurate information. The time for
this process was minimized as SurveyMonkey had
built-in logic to make questions mandatory, which
allowed for only a defined set of answers and was set
to only allow one submission per participant. Once
the data review was completed, the spreadsheet was
saved for analysis. Researchers identified when 75%
of experts select 4 or 5 on a Likert-type scale,
consensus had been met (Diamond et al., 2014; Fox
et al., 2016; Paoloni et al., 2017). In performing this
methodical approach, the goal of this study was to
narrow the gap between the critical success factors
identified in the literature versus the critical success
factors employed in the field of ERP consulting.

Data Analysis Plan

Throughout the three rounds of the study, the
researcher analyzed the data to produce reliable
findings and to answer the research question and
sub-questions using an iterative approach (Kerwin-

Boudreau & Butler-Kisber, 2016). In this study, the researcher used the critical success factor conceptual framework as a tool to analyze the data. To reduce the time gap between Round 1 and Round 2 (once the panelists submitted Round 1 responses), the researcher began the data analysis process.

Round 1 survey responses were coded using the open-coding method. The open-coding method was used to categorize, sort through, and compare new critical success factors identified by participants (Iamratanakul, Badir, Siengthai, & Sukhotu, 2014; Remus, 2007). For narrative data, the researcher searched for common themes to group new critical success factors into thematic categories, given that thematic analysis was the most-used analysis tool in the first round of a Delphi study (Heitner et al., 2013). To organize data, the researcher used a spreadsheet to track participant responses and modifications. Once new critical success factors were categorized, if the top 10 most desirable critical success factors were not among the factors with the highest frequency, the lower-ranked factors were not added to critical success factors in Round 2's survey list.

Throughout data analysis, the researcher analyzed the numeric, Likert-type scale data. In the first round, the top 10 critical success factors with the highest desirability were moved to Round 2 of the study. The Round 2 data were comprised of the ERP manufacturing consultants' ratings of the desirability and feasibility of the top 10 most desirable critical success factors from Round 1 using two separate 5-point Likert-type scales. The researcher used a median score in Round 2 and only the top two percentages with a median score of 3.5 or higher on both the desirability and feasibility scales were included in Round 3. Round 3 data comprised the ERP manufacturing consultants' ratings of the remaining critical success factors for desirability and feasibility.

Demographic data were analyzed to describe the characteristics of the sample. For the nominal variables of gender and geographic region, the researcher described distribution of variables using the mode and frequency counts and percentages. For the ordinal variables of age, highest level of education attained, years of experience, and number of implementations completed in small- and medium-sized manufacturing environments, the researcher used frequency counts, percentages, and the mode.

The research question pertained to the level of consensus among ERP manufacturing consultants as to the desirability and feasibility of critical success factors for ERP implementations. To answer the research question and sub-questions, the critical success factors with the highest consensus on desirability were used to answer sub-question 1. The critical success factors with the highest feasibility were used to answer sub-question 2. The critical success factors with the highest consensus on both desirability and feasibility were used to answer the primary research question.

Issues of Trustworthiness

Qualitative studies consisted of credibility, transferability, dependability, and confirmability (Lincoln & Guba, 1985). Trustworthiness contributed to credibility of data elements, e.g., prolonged engagement, consistent observations, competence, participant checks, and debriefing (Abro, Khurshid, & Aamir, 2015).

Credibility

Reviewing different methodologies and frameworks enhanced the credibility of a research study (Denzin & Lincoln, 2005). Credibility in qualitative research was established when participants or reviewers of a study recognized experiences by reviewing the findings and could interpret the truth of the data (Cope, 2014; Lincoln & Guba, 1985). In this Delphi-based research study, the researcher identified ERP manufacturing consultants as a subject matter expert panel to validate the credibility of the research study. To ensure credibility, the findings of the study should have been aligned with reality (Shenton, 2004). Since ERP manufacturing consultants were found to be integral to the success of an ERP implementation (Ravasan & Mansouri, 2016; Rezania & Ouedraogo, 2013), the researcher chose this target population as the subject matter expert panel, given these resources were working directly with clients throughout the implementation lifecycle. The potential loss of objectivity led to credibility and trustworthiness concerns (Thomas & Magilvy, 2011). To ensure credibility and alleviate researcher bias, the researcher created a reflexive journal and ensured data saturation in the study.

Transferability

Transferability was used to describe how the knowledge generated in the resarch study was applied to similar groups or settings (Cope, 2014). To demonstrate transferability, the researcher attempted to establish a well-described study for the findings to be immediately put into practice at any phase of an ERP implementation. By using thick description of the critical success factors in the survey (Hasson & Keeney, 2011), the researcher's goal was to ensure transferability of data obtained from the Delphi research. By selecting ERP manufacturing consultants from a number of ERP providers, the results of the study may be transferable across all ERP platforms and implementation methodologies. With transferability, the results may be applied to other situations or contexts (Collier-Reed, Ingerman, & Berglund, 2009; Langley, 1999). Although the

study focused on ERP applications, the identified
critical success factors may also be transferred
outside of ERP applications. Outside of business
enterprises, governments and academic institutions
implement applications to enhance their decision-
making, management, and workflow capabilities. For
these non-ERP requirements, these organizations
can refer to the results of the current study to
understand the critical success factors exercised in
their Learning Management Systems (LMS) or
Customer Relationship Management (CRM) projects.

Dependability

Consistency in the problem statement, the
purpose statement, and the research question
improved the logic and transparency of research
(Newman & Covrig, 2013). Due to the iterative nature
of a Delphi study, continuous checks of the survey
data and participant responses were performed.
Alignment of the methodology to the problem
statement, the purpose statement, and the research
question supported dependability to ensure
consistency and transparency (Newman & Covrig,

2013). In performing quality assurance throughout the study, the researcher's goal was to help the reader trust the research. The researcher used an audit trail to assess trustworthiness in each round of this Delphi study (Carcary, 2009). The researcher created an audit trail of research notes during study construction, data gathering, data analysis, as well as feedback received from participants during the field test and Round 1.

Confirmability

The researcher used an audit trail and a reflexive journal to outline the life-cycle of the study to exercise confirmability. Using an audit trail in a Delphi study validated confirmability (Hasson & Keeney, 2011). The continuous maintenance of notes containing the rationale for decisions through the use of an audit trail enhanced the credibility of study (Cope, 2014; Glaser & Strauss, 2012). By creating a reflexive journal, the researcher ensured confirmability by documenting all steps and processes performed in the research study. In Appendix F, the researcher provided the reflexive journal used to track the methodological development, the design process, data collection experiences, and overall observations.

Ethical Procedures

Permissions. The researcher solicited participants for this study through topic-pertinent groups on LinkedIn. The researcher obtained permission from each LinkedIn group moderator to post the invitations for this research study. The researcher asked each LinkedIn moderator permission to post the survey invitation and URL link to the group. Prior to collecting any data, consent was obtained from each participant who chose to participate in the study.

Recruitment. No ethical concerns related to the recruitment of participants were known prior to conducting the study. The participants were anonymous and the researcher notified the LinkedIn moderators when to submit additional invitations for subsequent rounds of the study (see Appendix G). The invitation for the subsequent rounds of the study included the premise of the study, the informed consent and survey link, and a statement that noted the surveys after Round 1 were open only to participants that participated in the previous round.

Informed consent. Once the participants agreed to participate in the study and clicked on the link within the LinkedIn group, they were presented with an informed consent form as outlined in Appendix H. The researcher made the informed consent form easy to understand to allow each participant to assess the risks and benefits before agreeing to participate. The informed consent outlined the purpose, goals, the nature of the study, the estimated time to complete the study, and the expectations of the study. The document included a statement that encouraged study participants to contact the researcher with any questions. The informed consent noted participation in the study was voluntary and participants could have withdrawn at any time by not submitting the survey or refraining from participating in subsequent rounds.

The participants were notified they would not be compensated for participating in this study. Although there were no physical risks or threats in participating in this study, there were minimal risks that did not exceed a level that any participant encountered during normal daily activities or in routine completion of psychological tests. The potential benefit to this study was to build upon the body of knowledge of the ERP consulting practice to better support manufacturing business clients in the United States. The researcher explained the research could provide an opportunity to experience how a Delphi study was conducted.

Once participants read the form and selected the link indicating agreement to consent to participate, the participants were directed to the screening questions. The participant was then prompted to check yes or no in response to each question to verify self-selection based on the criteria provided in the invitation. Participants that selected no for any of the questions were thanked for their interest and were unable to access the survey. If they selected yes to all of the screening questions, they continued to Round 1 of the survey. Once a survey was submitted, data could not be withdrawn.

Anonymity

Safeguards were enacted to protect the anonymity of the research study participants. The research survey was administered through SurveyMonkey (programmed to not collect internet protocol (IP) addresses). SurveyMonkey used data encryption for their servers located in secured data centers across the United States (Awuah, 2015). In Appendix I, the URL was provided to SurveyMonkey policies and procedures for protecting confidentiality, privacy, and use of the data.

Chapter 4

Results

The purpose of this qualitative modified Delphi study was to identify a consensus among a panel of ERP manufacturing consultants as to the desirability and feasibility of critical success factors in ERP implementations in the United States. The results of this study reduced the gap between the critical success factors identified in the literature versus those applied in manufacturing environments. The answers to the research question and sub-questions filled the knowledge gap of critical success factors of ERP implementations.

RQ1: What is the level of consensus among ERP manufacturing consultants as to the feasibility and desirability of critical success factors for ERP implementations?

RQ1 Sub-question 1: What is the level of consensus among manufacturing consultants as to the feasibility of critical success factors for ERP implementations?

RQ1 Sub-question 2: What is the level of consensus among manufacturing consultants as to the desirability of critical success factors for ERP implementations?

Research Setting

This study involved finding participants who had experience implementing ERP applications in small- and medium-sized manufacturing enterprises in the United States. Given the researcher's experience implementing ERP applications in small- and medium-sized manufacturing environments, it was important to separate personal knowledge and experience from the study. Throughout each round of this study, the researcher integrated several approaches to bracket personal experience. During the data analysis in Round 1, the researcher used Moustakas' (1994) method to isolate invariant constituents and coded narrative data submitted by the study participants. No judgments were made as to what to include and remove during the coding process. The researcher was objective in data analysis and coding by creating thematic categories for new critical success factors identified by the study participants. The researcher categorized and sorted the critical success factors based on the participants' responses, not based on the researcher's empirical experience. Because the data were collected electronically, the researcher was unable to assess nor had knowledge of any conditions or environments that influenced the participants' participation in the study. Outside of the demographic questions and the participants' responses to the screening questions, no other personal information was collected.

Demographics

The participants for the study were selected based on the following criteria: (a) at least five years of experience implementing ERP applications, (b) experience performing ERP implementations in the United States, (c) experience performing ERP implementations in the industrial or manufacturing sector, and (d) experience performing ERP implementations for small- and medium-sized enterprises (firms that employ fewer than 500 employees). The ERP manufacturing consultants self-selected based on the criteria provided in the invitation and were prompted to check yes or no in response to each question. If they selected no for any of the questions, they were thanked for their interest and were no longer able to access the survey.

Demographic data were collected from the panel of experts. The demographic questions included (a) age range, (b) gender, (c) education level, (d) years of experience, (e) number of implementations completed in small- and medium-sized manufacturing environments (organizations that employ less than 500 employees), and (f) geographic region. The gender and geographic region variables were measured on a nominal scale, where age, highest education attained, years of experience, and the number of implementations completed were measured on an ordinal scale. Collecting demographic data allowed for the analysis of the differences in responses based on criteria such as

years of experience and the number of
implementations completed. The collection of
demographic data in data analysis provided
information and insight for future research.

The following tables displayed aggregated
demographic characteristics of the panelists. Table 2
indicated the age range of the panel of experts. The
two major age groups, 45 to 54 and 55 to 64,
indicated individuals with years of experience in
business management and leadership roles were
typically those that had led ERP implementation
projects in small- and medium-sized manufacturing
enterprises.

Table 2 - Age Range (N = 42)

Age	N	%
21 and under	0	0.00
22 to 34	2	4.76
35 to 44	6	14.29
45 to 54	15	35.71
55 to 64	16	38.10
65 and over	3	7.14

The second characteristic of the panel of
experts was gender. The demographic data showed
a disproportionately large percentage of male

panelists compared to female panelists. These
results may be a reflection of the gender gap in the
manufacturing industry. Along with mining,
construction, and agriculture, the manufacturing
industry showed some of the highest levels of
industrial gender segregation in the United States
(Blau & Kahn, 2017).

Table 3 - Gender (N = 42)

Gender	N	%
Male	32	76.19
Female	10	23.81

The third panelist characteristic was years of
experience. More than two-thirds of the panelists had
over 10 years of ERP implementation experience.
The data indicated the expert panel had extensive
ERP implementation experience and represented a
tenured group of manufacturing consultants.

Table 4 - Panelists' Years of Experience (N = 42)

Years	N	%
5 to 10 years	8	19.05
11 to 15 years	22	52.38
16 to 20 years	4	9.52
21 years or more	8	19.05

The fourth panelist characteristic was highest
education level. More than 80% of the participants
held a master's degree. Because of the financial,
operational, and technological acumen required to
implement an ERP solution successfully, this
percentage implied consultants were continually
furthering their education (and potentially training) to
share knowledge with clients during ERP
implementations and organizational change initiatives
(Jensen, 2006).

Table 5 - Panelists' Highest Education Level (N = 42)

Education	N	%
High school diploma	0	0.00
Bachelor's degree	8	19.05
Master's degree	34	80.95
Doctoral degree	0	0.00

The fifth panelist characteristic was the number
of implementations the participants had completed in

small- and medium-sized manufacturing
environments. Some of the screening questions
required the participants to have at least five years of
experience implementing ERP solutions. Roughly
85% of the participants had performed at least six
implementations in small- and medium-sized
enterprises.

*Table 6 - Participants' Implementations Completed in Small-
and medium-sized manufacturing Environments (N = 42)*

Number of implementations	n	%
1 to 5	6	14.29
6 to 10	18	42.86
11 to 15	7	16.67
16 to 20	6	14.29
20 or more	5	11.90

The sixth panelist characteristic was the
participants' geographic region. The highest
percentage of participants implementing ERP
solutions was in the Midwest. Data showed
manufacturing organizations in this region of the
United States were still investing in operations, even
though researchers noted declines in production in
the industrial Midwest (Hannigan, Cano-Kollmann, &
Mudambi, 2015; Low & Brown, 2017).

Table 7 - Participants' Geographic Region (N = 42)

Region	n	%
Northeast	11	26.19
Midwest	13	30.95
Southeast	6	14.29
Southwest	4	9.52
West	8	19.05

Participation Overview

Fifty-seven ERP manufacturing consultants who satisfied the selection criteria agreed to participate in the study by accepting the procedures outlined in the informed consent form. Of the 57 ERP manufacturing consultants who participated in Round 1, 51 participants provided usable surveys. Of the 51 consultants who participated in Round 1, 42 participated in all three rounds. Table 8 outlined the completion rate for each round of the study. Given the participants were anonymous, the researcher could not engage in any follow-up with participants who dropped out of the study. No indications suggested participants dropped out due to any concerns with the study, assumptions could be made that they did not enter the LinkedIn (sourced) group to

see the notices of next rounds of data collection
during the second round's time period.

Table 8 - Survey Response Rate for Each Round

Round	Surveys returned	Completed surveys	Completion rate	Attrition rate
	N	N	%	%
1	57	51	89.47	N/A
2	48	47	97.92	92.16
3	44	42	95.45	82.35

Location, Frequency, and Duration of Data Collection

Data collection took place between September
17, 2018 and October 31, 2018. The three data
collection instruments (rounds) used in this Delphi
study were distributed through SurveyMonkey. The
exchange of all three survey invitations were
distributed to LinkedIn moderators to post to their
respective LinkedIn groups. Although the researcher
allocated a week period to allow sufficient time for
data analysis, the data were analyzed within a day via

analysis tools within SurveyMonkey and SPSS to calculate descriptive statistics for the rating data. Table 9 outlined the data collection timeline for this study.

Table 9 - Data Collection Timeline

Activity	Start Date	End Date
Round 1 administration		
Analysis of	09/17/18	10/01/18
Round 1 data	10/01/18	10/02/18
Round 2 administration		
Analysis of	10/02/18	10/16/18
Round 2 data	10/16/18	10/17/18
Round 3 administration		
Analysis of	10/17/18	10/31/18
Round 3 data	11/02/18	11/03/18

Round 1. Round 1 data collection occurred between September 17, 2018 and October 1, 2018. Of the 57 surveys returned, only 51 surveys were usable due to incomplete questionnaires. Of the 51 usable surveys, the expert panel proposed 18 modifications to the critical success factors at the end of the Round 1 survey. As noted in Chapter 3, the researcher performed a field test of the Round 1 survey to receive feedback on the clarity and

relevance of the questions. One expert stated they needed to read the survey objective twice before understanding how to answer the survey questions. The researcher rephrased the objective to make it more understandable to the expert panel before Round 1 began. Regarding the definitions for the study, one of the experts stated they were somewhat unclear of the local vendor partnership metric. To resolve this issue, the researcher added definitions to the metrics to ensure the participants fully understood the critical success factor when taking the survey.

Round 2. Round 2 data collection of the study began immediately after analyzing and coding Round 1 data and extended from October 2, 2018 to October 16, 2018. The expert panel rated the top 10 most desirable critical success factors from Round 1 using two separate 5-point Likert-type scales: desirability and feasibility. In Round 2, the critical success factors with the top two percentages (rating of 4 or 5) with 75% or higher on both the desirability and feasibility scales were to be moved to Round 3. Eight out of the 10 critical success factors were the basis for the rating index in Round 3.

Round 3. In the third round that spanned from
October 17, 2018 to October 31, 2018, the expert
panel rated the critical success factors carried over
from the second round against the same two 5-point
Likert-type scales used in Round 2. The goal was to
build the level of consensus among the panelists as to
the desirability and feasibility of critical success
factors for ERP implementations.

Data Recording Procedures

The researcher distributed all three surveys to
the participants using SurveyMonkey. The data from
each round were compiled into a master password-
protected Microsoft Excel spreadsheet. Once Round
1 concluded, the researcher exported the data into a
spreadsheet and separated the non-narrative and
narrative data into separate tabs. At the conclusion of
Round 2 and Round 3, the data were exported out of
SurveyMonkey and transferred the data to the master
spreadsheet.

Variations in Data Collection

A few differences existed between the data collection plan outlined in Chapter 3 and the actual data collection performed for this study. As stated in Chapter 3, in Round 2, the critical success factors with the top two percentages (rating of 4 or 5) with 75% or higher and with a median score of 3.5 or higher on both the desirability and feasibility scales were to be moved to Round 3. Given the 10 critical success factors would move to Round 3 with both measures, the researcher removed the median score as the second measure of consensus, resulting in eight critical success factors moving to Round 3.

Data Analysis

Participants in this modified Delphi study completed three separate surveys over a 1.5-month period. The iterative 3-round Delphi approach led to data to analyze. The researcher analyzed the data with the tools SurveyMonkey and SPSS provided. The researcher used thematic analysis to categorize and sort the participants' responses in Round 1 of the study. The researcher initiated the process by creating a separate tab on a master spreadsheet to separate responses and modifications. In reviewing the narrative data, the researcher coded data develop a list of categories.

The researcher used the open-coding method to categorize and sort the proposed critical success factors. To scan for frequencies of phrases or themes, the researcher used the Textalyser application (http://textalyser.net) to analyze participant's responses. Out of 18 responses, five common themes were identified: (a) rewards and recognition, (b) realistic project scope, (c) extensive testing and sign-off (d) defined roles and responsibilities, and (e) extensive end-user training. Due to high frequencies of the rated critical success factors in the survey, the panelist-suggested additional success factors (which were not rated as high as the critical success factors) were not moved to Round 2.

Unlike Round 1, Rounds 2 and 3 did not include thematic analysis. Instead, numeric rating data were analyzed with SPSS to determine frequencies, the median, and internal consistency reliability of the scales. Aligned with the research study design, the researcher used percentage agreement to measure the consensus of the data in Round 2. The same measure of consensus of 75% was applied to Round 3. Upon completing Round 2, Cronbach's alpha was used to test the internal consistency reliability of the multipoint Likert scale. In this round, the value of 0.8 exceeded the acceptable reliability coefficient of 0.7 (Nunnally, 1967; Wijkstra et al., 1994). Cronbach's alpha measure indicated that overall, the Round 2 survey items were 80% reliable for rating the desirability and feasibility of the critical success factors identified in the study. Because Cronbach's alpha did not measure consistency and stability over time, Cronbach's alpha was used to test internal reliability in Round 3 (Godoe & Johansen, 2012).

In Round 3, the remaining eight critical success factors were analyzed. Referring back to the initial plan to include the median score with the percentage agreement, the median score became the tie-breaker for the research question and both sub-questions. In reviewing Cronbach's alpha, similar to Round 2, overall the Round 3 items were 80% reliable for rating

the desirability and feasibility of the critical success
factors. See Table 10 for Cronbach's alpha by item
for Rounds 2 and 3.

Table 10 - Reliability of Instruments by Item

Critical Success Factor	Desirability		Feasibility	
	Round 2 Cronbach's alpha	Round 3 Cronbach's alpha	Round 2 Cronbach's alpha	Round 3 Cronbach's alpha
Cultural change readiness	0.809	0.875	0.801	0.862
Top management support and commitment	0.805	0.881	0.799	0.884
ERP fit with the organization	0.810	0.873	0.789	0.872
Business process re-engineering	0.802	0.869	0.784	0.871
Quality management	0.805	0.874	0.797	0.876
Detailed data migration plan	0.782	0.873	0.771	0.860
Small internal team of the best employees	0.809	0.870	0.806	0.865
Open and transparent communication	0.793	0.873	0.783	0.877
Contingency plans	0.772		0.771	
User feedback usage	0.780		0.786	

Evidence of Trustworthiness

Credibility

There were no adjustments from the proposed credibility plan and the final credibility approach in this research study. Some participants provided more information regarding critical success factors than others in Round 1 of the study, but responses aligned with critical success factors and critical-failure factors reviewed in the literature. The researcher did not detect any instances of persons participating in any round of the study who did not participate in the previous round; the researcher did not have trustworthiness concerns with the participants' responses (Thomas & Magilvy, 2011).

Transferability

With the goal of enabling practitioners and researchers to apply the researcher's findings outside of ERP implementations, the researcher applied thick description of the critical success factors in the survey

(Hasson & Keeney, 2011). Although the critical success factors in this study focused on ERP implementations, the critical success factors could also be applied (transferability) to non-technical studies, such as business process-improvement initiatives and organizational-change initiatives, among other project-based deployments.

Dependability

The research to uncover and validate the critical success factors in small- and medium-sized manufacturing environments involved continuous checks of the survey data and participant responses. By using an audit trail to assess the trustworthiness in each round of this Delphi study, the researcher's goal helped the reader to trust the research (Carcary, 2009). As an additional measure of dependability, the researcher used Cronbach's alpha in Rounds 2 and 3 to examine the internal consistency reliability of multipoint scales (Heitner et al., 2013; Tavakol & Dennick, 2011). As described above, the Cronbach's alpha values exceeded the acceptable reliability coefficient of 0.7 (Nunnally, 1967; Wijkstra et al., 1994).

Confirmability

The researcher used an audit trail and a reflexive journal to outline the life-cycle of the study to exercise confirmability. The researcher used a reflexive journal to substantiate the confirmability and to track changes and modifications throughout the study. By using these tools, the researcher was able to interpret the data with minimal bias. The researcher's goal was to demonstrate transparency of data given their role in the research study,

Study Results

The purpose of this study was to identify a consensus among an expert panel of ERP manufacturing consultants as to the desirability and feasibility of critical success factors in ERP implementations in the United States. The goal of this research study was to narrow the scholar-practitioner gap. To fill this gap, the researcher looked to answer the following research question and sub-questions:

RQ1: What is the level of consensus among ERP manufacturing consultants as to the desirability and feasibility of critical success factors for ERP implementations?

RQ1 Sub-question 1: What is the level of consensus among ERP manufacturing consultants as to the desirability of critical success factors for ERP implementations?

RQ1 Sub-question 2: What is the level of consensus among ERP manufacturing consultants as to the feasibility of critical success factors for ERP implementations?

This research study included an extensive literature review and a qualitative modified Delphi study. The expert panel of ERP manufacturing consultants provided input based on their empirical experience that led to an understanding of the critical success factors associated with successful implementations in small- and medium-sized manufacturing environments. The results of each of the three rounds of the Delphi study were as follows:

Round 1. The responses indicated that quality management and detailed data migration plan and readiness were the most desirable critical success factors followed by top executive management support and commitment. Appendix J outlined the Round 1 non-narrative data results. In reviewing the data, given that 46 of the 51 panelists found top management support to be highly desirable, the one highly undesirable response for top management support and commitment appeared to be an outlier. If this assumption was true, the panelists reached an almost 100% consensus regarding desirability on quality management, detailed data migration planning and readiness, and top management support.

Regarding the critical success factors with the lowest levels of desirability, local vendor's partnership and legacy systems support ranked the lowest out of all 22 critical success factors with none of the panelists rating local vendor's partnership as highly desirable. Although 18 panelists viewed base-point analysis or benchmarking to be highly desirable, it was the third-lowest ranking critical success factor in

Round 1. Due to the frequencies of the critical success factors in the survey, these suggested critical success factors the participants suggested to add were not moved to Round 2. Of the 22 most desirable critical success factors rated in Round 1, the critical success factors moved to Round 2 were: (a) cultural change readiness, (b) top management support and commitment, (c) ERP fit with the organization, (d) business process re-engineering, (e) quality management, (f) detailed data migration plan, (g) small internal team of the best employees, (h) open and honest communication, (i) contingency plans, and (j) user feedback usage.

Round 2. Based on the results of the analysis of the Round 2 data, only the top two percentages of 75% or higher on both the desirability and feasibility scales were moved to Round 3. As in Round 1, top management support and commitment were the critical success factors with the highest consensus. When including feasibility in the survey, the consensus increased for the two factors of ERP fit in the organization and small internal team of the best employees. These two factors were directly connected to the top management support and commitment factor as leadership decisions directly affect the selection of the ERP application and the forming of the project teams for the implementation. Of the 10 critical success factors in this Round, two did not satisfy the consensus threshold: (a) contingency plans, and (b) user feedback usage. Table 11 outlined the results of Round 2.

Table 11 - Round 2 Results

Critical success factor	Desirability		Feasibility	
	Top two responses %	Median	Top two responses %	Median
Cultural change readiness	95.74	5.00	87.23	4.00
Top management support and commitment	100.00	5.00	100.00	5.00
ERP fit with the organization	100.00	4.00	95.75	4.00
Business process re-engineering	85.11	4.00	87.23	4.00
Quality management	91.49	5.00	97.87	4.00
Detailed data migration plan	89.36	5.00	87.23	5.00
Small internal team of the best employees	100.00	5.00	95.75	4.00

Critical success factor	Desirability		Feasibility	
	Top two responses %	Median	Top two responses %	Median
Open and transparent communication	78.12	4.00	85.11	4.00
Contingency plans	80.85	4.00	70.21	4.00
User feedback usage	85.11	4.00	72.34	4.00

Round 3. Of the eight critical success factors, all met the threshold for inclusion in the final list of critical success factors. Table 12 outlined the results of Round 3. The consensus for the desirability and feasibility of the top critical success factor of top management support and commitment remained the same through all rounds of the study. Also, similar to Round 2, the ERP fit within the organization was of the highest-rated critical success factors in Round 3.

Table 12 - Round 3 Results

Critical success factor	Desirability		Feasibility	
	Top two responses %	Median	Top two responses %	Median
Cultural change readiness	95.24	5.00	85.71	4.00
Top management support and commitment	100.00	5.00	100.00	5.00
ERP fit with the organization	100.00	4.00	100.00	4.00
Business process re-engineering	85.71	4.00	85.71	4.00
Quality management	90.47	5.00	97.61	4.00
Detailed data migration plan	88.10	5.00	85.71	5.00
Small internal team of the best employees	95.24	5.00	95.24	4.00
Open and transparent communication	78.57	4.00	83.33	4.00

Consensus of responses for Research Sub-question 1. Research Sub-question 1 pertained to the level of desirability of critical success factors in ERP implementations. The original cutoff for consensus was set at 75% based on the literature (Diamond et al., 2014; Fox et al., 2016; Paoloni et al., 2017). Because there was a high level of consensus

for all eight critical success factors, the researcher
increased the cutoff to 90%. As shown in Table 13,
the panelists reached 90% consensus on the level of
desirability of the following five critical success
factors: (a) cultural-change readiness, (b) top
management support and commitment, (c) ERP fit
with the organization, (d) quality management, and (e)
a small internal team of the best employees. The
panelists reached 100% consensus on desirability for
both top management support and commitment and
ERP fit with the organization. Top management
support and commitment had the highest median of
5.00, resulting in the factor with the highest level of
consensus on desirability.

**Consensus of responses for Research Sub-
question 2.** Research Sub-question 2 pertained to
the level of feasibility of critical success factors in
ERP implementations. As with desirability, the
panelists reached 100% consensus on feasibility for
both top management support and commitment and
ERP fit with the organization. The median score was
5.00 for top management support and commitment,
indicating this factor had the highest level of

consensus for feasibility. Consistent with the
approach used for desiraability, the researcher
increased the cutoff for consensus on feasibility to
90%. As depicted in Table 13, the panelists reached
90% consensus on feasibility of the following four
critical success factors: (a) top management support
and commitment, (b) ERP fit with the organization, (c)
quality management, and (d) a small internal team of
the best employees.

**Consensus of responses for the Research
Question.** The primary research question pertained
to the level of desirability and feasibility of critical
success factors in ERP implementations. Table 13
depicted the four critical success factors on which the
expert panelists reached 90% consensus on the
levels of desirability and feasibility: (a) top
management support and commitment, (b) ERP fit
with the organization, (c) quality management, and (d)
a small internal team of the best employees. Top
management support and commitment was the critical
success factor with the highest consensus for
desirability and feasibility, followed closely by ERP fit
with the organization.

Summary

The three rounds of this qualitative modified Delphi study were the result of an effort to identify a consensus among a panel of ERP manufacturing consultants as to the desirability and feasibility of critical success factors in ERP implementations in the United States. The panel of ERP manufacturing consultants rated items for desirability and feasibility during the three rounds of the study and were asked to provide their expert opinions to reach consensus.

Chapter 5

Discussion, Conclusions, and Recommendations

The purpose of this qualitative modified Delphi study was to identify a consensus among an expert panel of ERP manufacturing consultants as to the desirability and feasibility of critical success factors in ERP implementations in the United States. The study included three rounds of surveys with 42 voluntary participants with extensive experience implementing ERP applications in small- and medium-sized manufacturing environments in the United States. Data were collected using Likert-type surveys and the data analyzed using computer assisted analysis (via SurveyMonkey, SPSS, and a Textalyser application [http://textalyser.net]). The critical success factors with the highest consensus on the levels of desirability and feasibility were top management support and commitment, ERP fit with the organization, quality management, and a small internal team of the best employees. Top management support and commitment had the highest consensus, followed closely by ERP fit with the organization.

Interpretation of Findings

The results of the study were conceptualized through the critical success factor framework. This study was framed around a primary research question: What is the level of consensus among ERP manufacturing consultants as to the desirability and feasibility of critical success factors for ERP implementations? The critical success factors with the highest consensus on the levels of desirability and feasibility were top management support and commitment, ERP fit with the organization, quality management, and a small internal team of the best employees. Top management support and commitment had the highest consensus, followed closely by ERP fit with the organization.

As outlined in Chapter 4, the expert panel reached 100% consensus that leadership support and commitment and ERP fit with the organization were the highest rated critical success factors among the eight rated in Round 3 and the original 22 reviewed in this study regarding to desirability and feasibility.

Top management support and commitment. Leadership support is a critical success factor in which many researchers have reached consensus (Aldholay, Isaac, Abdullah, & Ramayah, 2018; Loonam, Kumar, Mitra, & Abd Razak, 2018; Shao et al., 2016). The research findings indicate the panel of ERP manufacturing subject matter experts found it desirable and feasible to have top management support and commitment to successful implement a solution in small- and medium-sized manufacturing environments. In defining top management support and commitment as the company-wide support of empowered decision makers, leaders should not view an ERP implementation as a technology project, the implementation should be viewed as a strategic company initiative. In reviewing the final results, the responses from expert panel of manufacturing consultants were aligned with the body of literature. Although the study results of the study converge with the body of literature, researchers have differing views of leadership approaches to implement during times of organizational change.

Although cultural change readiness met the minimum level of desirability, this critical success factor did not meet the minimum feasibility criteria in the final round; however, cultural change readiness is also aligned with top management support and commitment. While leaders assess the risks associated with large organizational changes, a cultural assessment may be required before embarking on a large project. With the level of change of an ERP implementation, some leaders encounter resistance from their workforce, which may require a change in leadership approach. Leadership effectiveness increases the probability of an organization to change (Aarons, Ehrhart, Farahnak, & Hurlburt, 2015). Researchers indicated an absence of a one-size-fits-all change management approach (Hamstra, Yperen, Wisse, & Sassenberg, 2013; Wang & Zhu, 2010). Researchers outlined transformational leadership as a preferred approach over transactional leadership (García-Morales et al., 2012; Grant, 2012), but transactional leadership still has its place in organizational environments.

In business environments, employees are empowered by the transformational leadership characteristics the project provides through the means of decision-making opportunities (Elkhani et al., 2014), while other employees look to be rewarded for participating in the change initiative (Joia et al., 2014). Cullinane, Bosak, Flood, and Demerouti, (2017) stated standardized, lean practices could lead to reduced job enrichment and engagement among employees. Maas et al. (2014) argued against Cullinane et al.'s finding by indicating reduced job enrichment and engagement could be mitigated by engaging employees in the implementation of these business process re-engineering and lean initiatives. To validate Maas et al.'s finding, Chow (2018) found employees are empowered and motivated to make a positive impact on the organization, leading to increased innovation and creativity in the workplace.

Small internal team of the best employees. In creating cross-functional teams of the organization's best employees, leaders can harness the innovative thoughts of the employee base to build ideas organically and create a knowledge-sharing environment. The literature indicates a servant leadership style can enable leaders to help employees contribute to the overall organizational vision (Flynn et al., 2015). Servant leaders are more empathetic and incorporate EI; with EI, servant leadership enhances leadership competencies by promoting the strengths of others. In tying the small internal team of the organization's best employees with open and transparent communication, employee decision making can be increased by developing information communication channels. In providing these small teams with tools to be successful, leaders assist their employees in making decisions to benefit all parties, including the organization, by displaying open, honest communication.

When developing the group of the organization's best employees, leaders can assess the leadership competencies of each group member. Shared leadership enables team members to express different abilities and opinion in a decision-making process, enabling different, individual, decision-making styles (Bergman, Rentsch, Small, Davenport, & Bergman, 2012). By instituting shared leadership practices, leaders of organizations can increase the trust, collaboration, and autonomy among team members, even after a project or initiative is completed (Ulhøi & Müller, 2014).

Enterprise Resource Planning fit with the organization. Technology increases communication and visibility among organizations, resulting in a shift in managerial approaches to remain competitive in respective markets. Research study findings align with the literature. In a survey of 169 IT leaders regarding users' resistance to enterprise applications, Joia et al. (2014) conclude leaders can mitigate resistance by ensuring applications are well designed, are easy to use, and have simple interfaces. To ensure ERP fit within an organization, leaders and software providers incorporate collective intelligence by creating new functionality within the new ERP application (Kim & Altmann, 2013). A collaborative approach leads to increased user satisfaction and adoption of new technology.

Culture is perceived as organizational core values, assumptions, and interpretations; the link between employees and culture is apparent (Borgogni, Russo, & Latham, 2010). Leaders introduce strategies and goals, but followers refine and make strategies relevant. Leaders who adapt this thinking attribute organizational success to positive group norms and form normative ties with employees (Harms & Crede, 2010). In the research literature, although leadership approaches are successfully implemented in business environments, the selected approach depends upon the objective.

Trust, an often-overlooked component to successfully implement change, is a critical factor among stakeholders. For effective relationships to be created, nurtured, and propagated, trust must be distributed within the organization to build team spirit by demonstrating open and transparent communication throughout the project lifecycle (Le Pennec & Raufflet, 2016). Leaders should foster an atmosphere in which trust and respect thrive and innovation flourishes in building a learning organization necessary for sustainable development (Kareem, 2016). To make a positive impact on the corporation's environment and community, leaders of organizations must assess the key variables for success before acting upon an organizational change.

**Quality management and a detailed
migration plan.** Research study findings converge
with the literature. To address the issue that
technological fit alone will lead to a competitive
advantage for leaders of organizations, Goodhue and
Thompson (1995) created a task-technology fit (TTF)
model to ensure a positive influence on individual
performance. Goodhue and Thompson created an
instrument to measure eight factors: (a) data quality,
(b) locate-ability, (c) authorization, (d) compatibility,
(e) timeliness, (f) reliability, (g) ease of training, and
(h) relationship. The current study findings about the
critical success factors of detailed data migration plan
and quality management fit into the data quality
factors that Goodhue and Thompson measured.

Tripathi and Jigeesh (2015) used the TTF
model to evaluate the fit and adoption of a cloud
computing solution in an organization, concluding if
leaders of organizations institute a detailed data
migration plan, including audits throughout the data
cleansing and conversion process, users of the
organization incur a high level of data quality in the
business application, resulting in an increase in
productivity. The TTF model has been modified or

used in conjunction with other models such as technology acceptance model (TAM) and the unified theory of acceptance and use of technology (UTAUT) model (Davis, Bagozzi, & Warshaw, 1989; Venkatesh, Morris, Davis, & Davis, 2003; Zigurs & Buckland, 1998). Researchers continue to use the TTF model in studies to measure workplace system fit, usage, and performance.

Of the eight critical success factors rated for desirability and feasibility in the final round, only two focused on the technological aspect: ERP fit with the organization and a detailed migration plan. Given the remaining six factors – cultural change readiness, ERP fit with the organization, business process re-engineering, quality management, a small team of the best employees, and open and transparent communication – focused on people or process, the current study findings could positively influence social change by applying these critical success factors to organizational change initiatives.

Limitations of the Study

The study had potential limitations. Due to the iterative nature of Delphi studies, attrition is always a risk (Gray, 2016; McMillan et al., 2016). Although there were no indications the panelists dropped out of the study due to its duration, the voluntary nature of the study limited the researcher's access to reasons panelists dropped out of subsequent study rounds. Another limitation of the study was the original consensus threshold, which was set at 75% based on the literature (Diamond et al., 2014; Fox et al., 2016; Paoloni et al., 2017). The high level of consensus for the eight critical success factors in Round 3 led to increasing the cutoff to 90% for desirability and feasibility to determine which critical success factors most desirable and feasible among the panelists.

The purposive sampling technique was also a limitation of this study. Although the panelists met the researcher's selection criteria, the selection of ERP manufacturing consultants could have been too narrow a scope. The blending of consulting and project manager roles in the study may have provided a different perspective, resulting in identification of new critical success factors in Round 1 given that individuals, such as project managers, may have previous consulting experience,

The self-selected expert panel of ERP manufacturing consultants within the United States did not include ERP manufacturing consultants from outside the United States geographical area. Selecting ERP manufacturing consultants from other countries may have produced different results due to varying cultures, work environments, and leadership styles. García-Sánchez and Pérez-Bernal (2007) found in countries such as China and Mexico, leaders do not use decision-support systems such as ERP applications; rather, leaders follow cultural traditions of experience and intuition to make business decisions. Leaders in countries facing difficulty implementing western technologies may be due to technological infrastructure or the skill level of the employee base. Avison and Malaurent (2007) cautioned consultants and software vendors to be aware of cultural differences in other countries.

Another limitation to the study was the researcher used a previously established list of 22 consolidated critical success factors to conduct the survey. Although the researcher allowed the expert panel of ERP manufacturing consultants to provide additional factors not outlined in the survey, there was the potential risk of influence and bias, given the researcher provided the panelists with a list of critical success factors. The methods used in this study should be transferrable, not only in ERP implementations, but for non-ERP projects as well, including Learning Management Systems (LMS) or Customer Relationship Management (CRM) applications.

Recommendations

Modifications to Methodology and Design

The Delphi study was limited by the experience and expertise of the subject matter expert panelists. The study is also limited by the application of qualitative modified Delphi approach. This limitation could be addressed by implementing a quantitative or mixed methods Delphi approach or a design different from Delphi. A quantitative or mixed methods approach for the current Delphi study could expand the scope of the panel to a more heterogeneous group, such as project managers, end-users, and the organization's implementation teams. This qualitative modified Delphi approach may provide additional insight to the cultural or organizational challenges different groups face throughout the implementation lifecycle.

Changes to the Theory and Model

In the literature, Christensen and Raynor (2003) identified three purposes of theories: (a) to pinpoint causation, (b) to move toward predictability, and (c) to assist in analyzing successes and failures. Prior qualitative research has generated theories pertinent to organizational environments (Turner, 2014). In reviewing the literature, the common theory cited among ERP critical success factors is DeLone and McLean's (1992, 2003) information systems (IS) success model (Mwayongo & Omar, 2017; Siricha & Theuri, 2016). The DeLone and McLean IS success model is the most adopted and most cited theory in information systems research (Mudzana & Maharaj, 2015; Zouine & Fenies, 2015). DeLone and McLean

(2003) provided an update to their original model to respond to the change and progression that occurred across the IS landscape after the publication of their seminal work. Researchers have updated the DeLone and McLean (2003) model with various modifications to fit different information systems' environments and cultures. With DeLone and McLean's update to the model, other commonly cited studies focused on the re-specification and extension of the DeLone and McLean (1992) success model (Seddon, 1997; Seddon & Kiew, 1996). Although researchers who refuted the original model aimed to provide more theoretically sound studies, the DeLone and McLean model (1992) continues to outperform the modified models (Mudzana & Maharaj, 2015; Petter & McLean, 2009; Rai, Lang, & Welker, 2002; Stocker & Müller, 2016).

In addition to theories used to measure ERP the success of ERP implementations in small- and medium-sized environments, more models were identified. Models such as petri nets, decision trees, fuzzy cognitive maps, and causal models have been used to measure critical success factors by modelling the interrelations with people, processes, and technology (Gajic et al., 2014). The balanced scorecard model was the most cited model in the literature (Gajic et al., 2014; Fu, Chang, Ku, Chang, & Huang, 2014; Shen et al., 2016; Uwizeyemungu & Raymond, 2009). The balanced scorecard model is used to monitor financial and business processes, but could be used in ERP implementations to align vision, objectives, and measures throughout an ERP implementation lifecycle (Shen et al., 2016). First introduced by Kaplan and Norton (1996), the scorecard model could also be used in ERP implementations to define multi-dimensional features and potential effects throughout the entire project lifecycle. Shen et al. (2016) concluded, the primary objective for a balanced scorecard is to transform the visions of leaders of an organization into strategies and measures, using the balanced scorecard as a tool to build strategic processes, objectives, and measures, which takes a different approach to successfully implementing ERP applications.

Focus on Small- and Medium-Sized Enterprises in Different Industries

An additional analysis that focuses on this population may be required given small- and medium-sized enterprises made up a large portion of the employer firms in the United States. As outlined in Chapter 1, small- and medium-sized enterprises may face greater challenges in adopting technology as compared to large enterprises (Ghobakhloo et al., 2012). Because ERP research has been focused on large enterprises (Conteh & Akhtar, 2015; Maas et al., 2014; Mo & He, 2015), studies that focus on small- and medium-sized enterprises outside of the manufacturing industry may benefit other organizations. Given leaders of firms will most likely take part in only a few ERP implementations during their career, reviewing the results of firms regardless of industry may assist in alleviating potential issues arising during implementation.

Research That Builds on This Study's Findings

Recommendations for leadership. The current study supported and expanded upon the literature on the critical success factors in ERP implementations in small- and medium-sized manufacturing enterprises. Researchers concluded when top management works closely with ERP users, the communication between business groups is enhanced, and conflict resolution becomes attainable (Maditinos et al., 2012). Iveroth (2016) stated leaders of organizations should invest at least 50% of the budget of a technology project for establishing future state processes, training, education, and communication. To remain competitive in the market, firms must provide open, transparent communication and structures to spawn innovation (Chenhall, Kallunki, & Silvola, 2011). By maintaining close relationships internally – as well as externally – stakeholders involved will be able to assist in the innovation of the products and services of a technology and professional services organization.

Expert panelists in this research study identified leadership competencies needed to

successfully implement these ERP installations.
During ERP implementations, personnel within
organizations require process changes, leadership,
and change management (Conceição & Altman,
2011). During this process, leaders should build
learning organizations. Learning organizations are
organizations with individuals who focus on: (a) a
shared vision, (b) systems thinking, (c) mental
models, (d) team learning, and (e) personal mastery
(Senge, 1990). In creating learning organizations
during times of change, employees are empowered to
learn, creating a larger probability for employees to
embrace change (Benson, 2016). Learning
organizations enable stakeholders to remain current
on technological advances, providing benefits to both
the individual and the organization (Lozano, 2014).
Using these characteristics, during times of change
within an organization, may provide immense benefits
by harnessing innovative and creative ideas
implemented into new organizational processes and
procedures.

Recommendations for researchers. As the
implementation base for ERP integrations (e.g.,

blockchain technology) continues to grow, the critical success factors outlined in this study may require reassessment for small- and medium-sized manufacturing enterprises. With this research study focusing on internal commitment, collaboration, accountability, and trust, additional research may be required to assess the validity of existing critical success factors when an organization includes additional business partners and applications into the implementation. With this decentralized decision making (DDM) model, the critical success factors identified in this research study move outside of an organization's four walls (Marques, Agostinho, Zacharewicz, & Jardim-Gonçalves, 2017).

With ERP blockchain integrations, transactions are visible to all network participants, increasing the auditability, trust, and increasing the confidence in the data (Gromovs & Lammi, 2017; Li et al., 2018). As time and volume make the blockchain ledger more secure, more users within organizations may begin to transact immediate contracts, orders, and payments, essentially eliminating payment terms and increasing cash flow (Dai & Vasarhelyi, 2017; Wang, Wu, Wang, & Shou, 2017). Similar to the introduction of cloud computing, 3-D printing, Industry 4.0, and IoT, it comes down to education and knowledge sharing of blockchain capabilities before it is universally adopted.

Implications

Significance to Social Change

The researcher was able to identify a consensus among a panel of ERP manufacturing consultants of critical success factors both academic scholars and practitioners can implement into business environments. Putting the critical success factors into practice in ERP implementations could lead to the development of increased team collaboration, education, or other continuous improvement initiatives through: (a) leadership training for organization executives; (b) an established change management plan for large organizational changes; (c) unbiased education to understand the requirements and expectations to successfully implement an ERP solution; and, (d) an established internal project management office (PMO) to track the status, cost, and quality of organizational initiatives.

Although little research has been performed on the topic, ERP applications can enable leaders to improve their TBL. By providing visibility throughout a firm's global supply chain, these applications can track the usage of raw materials and ensure the firm's facilities are remaining environmentally responsible (Turner, 2014). For the people perspective of the TBL, researchers have found the implementation phase of ERP applications has led to empowerment, job enrichment, and innovative behavior (Krog & Govender, 2015b; Maas et al., 2014). Research has shown 80% of the Fortune 500 companies have implemented these solutions for improved decision-making and higher profitability, given that ERP applications integrated into the operational and financial functions of an organization (Maas et al., 2014). Leaders could promote positive social change by providing additional job opportunities and higher wages due to increased efficiencies by leveraging ERP applications.

While this study focused on ERP implementations in small- and medium-sized manufacturing environments, the results can have a

positive impact on social change in other industries
such as healthcare, hospitality, and education.
Although the applications in these industries have
different functions and serve different purposes, the
critical success factors outlined in this research study
could also be applied to hospitality management
systems, healthcare management systems, and
learning management systems. Because industries
previously mentioned operate in different
environments and cultures than manufacturers, the
unconventional view of software implementations as it
pertains to small- and medium-sized manufacturing
could lead to positive social change by viewing the
software implementation through a different lens.

Significance to Theory

A review of the literature in Chapter 2
uncovered the goal of researchers to identify critical
success factors is to provide benefits and create a
sustainable competitive advantage for leaders of
organizations. The literature also outlines the benefits
of identifying and managing critical success factors
throughout the ERP implementation lifecycle (Ram &

Corkindale, 2014). Similar to the iterative approach of a Delphi study, given technology is continually evolving and improving, and every iteration of critical success factors benefits the body of knowledge.

Significance to Practice

When embarking on a large endeavor such as an ERP implementation, leaders of business organizations may encounter resistance when implementing changes. These leaders should recognize ways employees could embrace change to mitigate the risk of failed implementations (Bordia, Restubog, Jimmieson, & Irmer, 2011). As organizations expanded across the country and the world, firms also experienced differing environmental cultures. Latta (2009) outlined the importance of identifying sub-cultures within an organization's system where resistance may arise. To validate this finding, an American manufacturer that had expanded to Spain uncovered the top five challenges within the new facility, with employee resistance to change tied for first along with the lack of technical knowledge of the employee base (Gil, Ruiz, Escrivá, Font, &

Manyes, 2017). During times of change, employees
look back on previous experiences, and poor change
management history (PCMH) can influence employee
perceptions of organizational change (Bordia et al.,
2011). With this finding, leaders must look outside of
conventional leadership methods to alleviate the risk
of resistance. Adoption of change can uncover
advantages among stakeholders within an
organization by becoming proactive in identification of
resistance.

Trust is a critical factor among stakeholders,
yet this factor is overlooked when implementing
change. For effective relationships to be created,
nurtured, and propagated, trust must be distributed
within the organization to build team spirit (Gillespie &
Mann, 2004). Leaders should foster an atmosphere
in which trust and respect thrive and innovation
flourishes in building a learning organization, which is
necessary for sustainable development (Kareem,
2016). To make a positive influence on the
corporation's environment and community, leaders of
organizations much first assess the key variables for
success before acting upon the organizational change
initiative.

Regardless of the approach, providing transparency at the departmental level to gain buy-in to implement change at that level will encourage input from lower level personnel during the change initiative (Sikdar & Payyazhi, 2014). Once the change is rolled out at the organizational level, leaders can create a holistic, organic environment that leads to innovative actions and decision-making (Sikdar & Payyazhi, 2014). When cultural change is perceived as an organization's core values, assumptions, and interpretations, the link between employees and culture is apparent (Borgogni et al., 2010). Leaders introduce strategies and goals, but followers refine these strategies and make them relevant. Leaders, who can adapt this form of thinking, will attribute organizational success to positive group norms and will form normative ties with employees (Harms & Crede, 2010). In reviewing the literature, although the leadership approaches are successfully implemented in a variety of environments, the selected approach depends upon the objective.

Conclusions

This research study introduced the general problem that ERP implementation failures continue to occur at a high rate in the manufacturing industry and the specific problem of the desirability and feasibility of conventional ERP implementation critical success factors may require reassessment among small- and medium-sized manufacturers (Alharthi et al., 2017; Hughes et al., 2016; Maas et al., 2014; Ram & Corkindale, 2014; Turner et al., 2016). The goal of this modified Delphi study was to reach a consensus among a group of experts as to the desirability and feasibility of critical success factors in ERP implementations in the United States. Of the original 22 critical success factors in Round 1, the panel of experts reached 90% consensus on the level of desirability and feasibility on four critical success factors: (a) top management support and commitment, (b) ERP fit with the organization, (c) quality management, and (d) a small internal team of the best employees. Top management support and commitment had the highest consensus, followed closely by ERP fit with the organization.

Answers to this study's research questions led to a number of conclusions as outlined in the interpretations section of this chapter. Leaders typically refer to their cognitive abilities to make decisions, and ERP applications could assist them in making those decisions typically performed with the lack of information. Although users utilize Excel spreadsheets and disparate systems, by installing a system that brings data into a centralized application, leaders, teams, and departments can collaborate, share data, and make better-informed decisions.

The results of the study are important to the fields of leadership and enterprise applications as the findings build on the body of knowledge for both disciplines. Regardless of the size of the organization, knowledge sharing is important both upstream and downstream. Leaders can benefit from this study to applying the new knowledge from this study within their organizations during times of change. Practitioners in the ERP industry can benefit from this study's findings by applying approaches outlined during ERP implementations to mitigate risk during these engagements.

REFERENCES

Aarons, G. A., Ehrhart, M. G., Farahnak, L. R., & Hurlburt, M. S. (2015). Leadership and organizational change for implementation (LOCI): A randomized mixed method pilot study of a leadership and organizational development intervention for evidence-based practice implementation. *Implementation Science, 10*(11), 11-26. doi:10.1186/s13012-014-0192-y

Abdelmoniem, E. M. (2016). The critical success factors and the effect of ERP system implementation on business performance: Case study in Egyptian environment. *International Journal of Computer Science and Information Security, 14*(5), 104-115. doi:10.20943/01201603.6677

Abdinnour, S., & Saeed, K. (2015). User perceptions towards an ERP system: Comparing the post-implementation phase to the pre-implementation phase. *Journal of Enterprise Information Management, 28*(2), 243-259. doi:10.1108/jeim-10-2013-0075

Abelein, U., & Paech, B. (2013). Understanding the influence of user participation and involvement on system success – a systematic mapping study. *Empirical Software Engineering, 20*(1), 28–81. doi:10.1007/s10664-013-9278-4

Abro, M. M. Q., Khurshid, M. A., & Aamir, A. (2015). The use of mixed methods in management research. *Journal of Applied Finance and Banking, 5*(2), 103-108. Retrieved from https://www.scienpress.com/

Ab Talib, M. S., & Abdul Hamid, A. B. (2014). Application of critical success factors in supply chain management. *International Journal of Supply Chain Management, 3*(1), 21-33. Retrieved from http://ojs.excelingtech.co.uk/index.php/IJSCM

Ab Talib, M. S., Abdul Hamid, A. B., & Thoo, A. C. (2015). Critical success factors of supply chain management: A literature survey and Pareto analysis. *EuroMed Journal of Business, 10*(2), 234–263. doi:10.1108/emjb-09-2014-0028

Acar, A. Z. (2012). Organizational culture, leadership styles and organizational commitment in Turkish logistics industry. *Procedia-Social and Behavioral Sciences, 58*(1), 217-226. doi:10.1016/j.sbspro.2012.09.995

Adler, M., & Ziglio, E. (1996). *Gazing into the oracle: The Delphi method and its application to social policy and public health*. London, England: Jessica Kingsley Publishers.

Aengenheyster, S., Cuhls, K., Gerhold, L., Heiskanen-Schüttler, M., Huck, J., & Muszynska, M. (2017). Real-time Delphi in practice—A comparative analysis of existing software-based tools. *Technological Forecasting and Social Change, 118*(2), 15-27. doi:10.1016/j.techfore.2017.01.023

Ahmad, N., & Mehmood, R. (2015). Enterprise systems: Are we ready for future sustainable cities. *Supply Chain Management: An International Journal, 20*(3), 264-283. doi:10.1108/scm-11-2014-0370

Akca, Y., & Ozer, G. (2014). Diffusion of innovation theory and an implementation on enterprise resource planning systems. *International Journal of Business and Management, 9*(4), 92-114. doi:10.5539/ijbm.v9n4p92

Aldholay, A. H., Isaac, O., Abdullah, Z., & Ramayah, T. (2018). The role of transformational leadership as a mediating variable in DeLone and McLean information system success model: The context of online learning usage in Yemen. *Telematics and Informatics, 35*(5), 1421-1437. doi:10.1016/j.tele.2018.03.012

Al-Haddad, S., & Kotnour, T. (2015). Integrating the organizational change literature: A model for successful change. *Journal of Organizational Change Management, 28*(2), 234-262. doi:10.1108/jocm-11-2013-0215

Alharthi, A., Alassafi, M. O., Walters, R. J., & Wills, G. B. (2017). An exploratory study for investigating the critical success factors for cloud migration in the Saudi Arabian higher education context. *Telematics and Informatics, 34*(2), 664-678. doi:10.1016/j.tele.2016.10.008

Ali, M., & Miller, L. (2017). ERP system implementation in large enterprises – a systematic literature review. *Journal of Enterprise Information Management, 30*(4), 666–692. doi:10.1108/jeim-07-2014-0071

Al-Johani, A. A., & Youssef, A. E. (2013). A framework for ERP systems in SME based on cloud computing technology. *International Journal on Cloud Computing: Services and Architecture, 3*(3), 1-14. doi:10.5121/ijccsa.2013.3301

Alshardan, A., Goodwin, R., & Rampersad, G. (2015). A benefits assessment model of information systems for small organizations in developing countries. *Computer and Information Science, 9*(1), 1-20. doi:10.5539/cis.v9n1p1

Althonayan, M., & Althonayan, A. (2017). E-government system evaluation: The case of users' performance using ERP systems in higher education. *Transforming Government: People, Process and Policy, 11*(3), 306-342. doi:10.1108/tg-11-2015-0045

Amba, S. M., & Abdulla, H. (2014). The impact of enterprise systems on small and medium-sized enterprises in the kingdom of Bahrain. *International Journal of Management and Marketing Research, 7*(1), 49-57. Retrieved from http://www.theibfr.com/ijmmr.htm

Anderson, J. C., & Gerbing, D. W. (1988). Structural equation modeling in practice: A review and recommended two-step approach. *Psychological bulletin, 103*(3), 411-423. doi:10.1037//0033-2909.103.3.411

Atkinson, N. L., & Gold, R. S. (2001). Online research to guide knowledge management planning. *Health Education and Research, 16*(6), 747-763. doi:10.1093/her/16.6.747

Avison, D., & Malaurent, J. (2007). Impact of cultural differences: A case study of ERP introduction in China. *International Journal of Information Management, 27*(5), 368–374. doi:10.1016/j.ijinfomgt.2007.06.004

Avots, I. (1969). Why does project management fail? *California Management Review, 12*(1), 77–82. doi:10.2307/41164208

Awuah, L. J. (2015). Supporting 21st-century teaching and learning: The role of Google apps for education (GAFE). *Journal of Instructional Research, 4*(1), 12-22. doi:10.9743/jir.2015.2

Azevedo, P. S., Romão, M., & Rebelo, E. (2014). Success factors for using ERP (enterprise resource planning) systems to improve competitiveness in the hospitality industry. *Tourism & Management Studies, 10*(2), 165-168. Retrieved from http://tmstudies.net/index.php/ectms

Banerjee, A. (2015). Information technology enabled process re-engineering for supply chain legality. *International Journal of Information Technology and Management, 14*(1), 60-75. doi:10.1504/ijitm.2015.066060

Bansal, V., & Agarwal, A. (2015). Enterprise resource planning: Identifying relationships among critical success factors. *Business Process Management Journal, 21*(6), 1337-1352. doi:10.1108/BPMJ-12-2014-0128

Basl, J. (2016). Enterprise information systems and technologies in Czech companies from the perspective of trends in industry 4.0. *Research and Practical Issues of Enterprise Information Systems, 10*(1), 156-165. doi:10.1007/978-3-319-49944-4_12

Baxter, G., & Sommerville, I. (2011). Socio-technical systems: From design methods to systems engineering. *Interacting with Computers, 23*(2), 4-17. doi:10.1016/j.intcom.2010.07.003

Baykasoğlu, A., & Gölcük, İ. (2017). Development of a two-phase structural model for evaluating ERP critical success factors along with a case study. *Computers & Industrial Engineering, 106*(1), 256-274. doi:10.1016/j.cie.2017.02.015

Beheshti, H. M., Blaylock, B. K., Henderson, D. A., & Lollar, J. G. (2014). Selection and critical success factors in successful ERP implementation. *Competitiveness Review, 24*(4), 357-375. doi:10.1108/cr-10-2013-0082

Belassi, W., & Tukel, O. I. (1996). A new framework for determining critical success/failure factors in projects. *International Journal of Project Management, 14*(3), 141–151. doi:10.1016/0263-7863(95)00064-x

Benson, D. (2016). Building the mental model for leadership. *Physician Leadership Journal, 3*(1), 48-50. Retrieved from https://www.physicianleaders.org/

Bento, A. [Al], Bento, R., & Bento, A. [Ana]. (2015). How fast are enterprise resource planning (ERP) systems moving to the cloud? *Journal of Information Technology Management, 26*(4), 35-44. Retrieved from https://jitm.ubalt.edu/

Bergman, J. Z., Rentsch, J. R., Small, E. E., Davenport, S. W., & Bergman, S. M. (2012). The shared leadership process in decision-making teams. *The Journal of Social Psychology, 152*(1), 17-42. doi:10.1080/00224545.2010.538763

Berman, J. (2013). Utility of a conceptual framework within doctoral study: A researcher's reflections. *Issues in Educational Research, 23*(1), 1-18. Retrieved from http://www.iier.org.au/iier.html

Bhuiyan, F., Chowdhury, M. M., & Ferdous, F. (2014). Historical evolution of human resource information system (HRIS): An interface between HR and computer technology. *Human Resource Management Research, 4*(4), 75-80. Retrieved from http://journal.sapub.org/hrmr

Bintoro, B. P. K., Simatupang, T. M., Putro, U. S., & Hermawan, P. (2015). Actors' interaction in the ERP implementation literature. *Business Process Management Journal, 21*(2), 222-249. doi:10.1108/bpmj-11-2013-0142

Blau, F. D., & Kahn, L. M. (2017). The gender wage gap: Extent, trends, and explanations. *Journal of Economic Literature, 55*(3), 789-865. doi:10.3386/w21913

Bohórquez, V., & Esteves, J. (2008). Analyzing SMEs as a moderator of ERP impact in SMEs' productivity. *Communications of the IIMA, 8*(3), 67-80. Retrieved from http://repositorio.ulima.edu.pe/

Bordia, P., Restubog, S. L. D., Jimmieson, N. L., & Irmer, B. E. (2011). Haunted by the past: Effects of poor change management history on employee attitudes and turnover. *Group Organization Management, 36*(2), 191-222. doi:10.1177/1059601110392990

Borgogni, L., Russo, S. D., & Latham, G. P. (2010). The relationship of employee perceptions of the immediate supervisor and top management with collective efficacy. *Journal of Leadership & Organizational Studies, 18*(1), 5-13. doi:10.1177/1548051810379799

Brady, S. R. (2015). Utilizing and adapting the Delphi method for use in qualitative research. *International Journal of Qualitative Methods, 14*(5), 1-6. doi:10.1177/1609406915621381

Bronnenmayer, M., Wirtz, B. W., & Göttel, V. (2016a). Determinants of perceived success in management consulting: An empirical investigation from the consultant perspective. *Management Research Review, 39*(6), 706-738. doi:10.1108/mrr-06-2014-0145

Bronnenmayer, M., Wirtz, B. W., & Göttel, V. (2016b). Success factors of management consulting. *Review of Managerial Science, 10*(1), 1-34. doi:10.1007/s11846-014-0137-5

Brumberg, R., Kops, E., Little, E., Gamble, G., Underbakke, J., & Havelka, D. (2016). Stalled ERP at random textiles. *Information Systems Education Journal, 14*(2), 49-57. Retrieved from http://isedj.org/

Burgess, S., Sellitto, C., Cox, C., & Buultjens, J. (2011). Trust perceptions of online travel information by different content creators: Some social and legal implications. *Information Systems Frontiers, 13*(2), 221-235. doi:10.1007/s10796-009-9192-x

Burkholder, G. J., Cox, K. A., & Crawford, L. M. (2016). *The scholar-practitioner's guide to research design.* Baltimore, MD: Laureate Publishing.

Burns, J. M. (1978). *Nursing and transformational leadership theory.* New York, NY: Harper & Row.

Carcary, M. (2009). The research audit trial – enhancing trustworthiness in qualitative inquiry. *The Electronic Journal of Business Research Methods, 7*(1), 11-24. Retrieved from http://www.ejbrm.com/

Carvalho, H. L., & Guerrini, F. M. (2017). Reference model for implementing ERP systems: An analytical innovation networks perspective. *Production Planning & Control 5*(17), 1-14. doi:10.1080/09537287.2016.1273409

Chang, J. Y. T., Wang, E. T. G., Jiang, J. J., & Klein, G. (2013). Controlling ERP consultants: Client and provider practices. *Journal of Systems & Software, 86*(5), 1453-1461. doi:10.1016/j.jss.2013.01.030

Chawla, A., & Sujatha, R. (2015). Explore, excite and expand leadership capacity lived experiences of present-day leaders on leadership training and development in India. *International Journal of Academic Research in Business and Social Sciences, 5*(9), 64-78. doi:10.6007/ijarbss/v5-i9/1814

Chen, L. (2010). Business–IT alignment maturity of companies in China. *Information & Management, 47*(1), 9-16. doi:10.1016/j.im.2009.09.003

Chen, S., Harris, L., Lai, J., & Li, W. (2016). ERP systems and earnings quality: The impact of dominant shareholdings in China. *Journal of Emerging Technologies in Accounting, 13*(2), 49-69. doi:10.2308/jeta-51547

Chenhall, R. H., Kallunki, J., & Silvola, H. (2011). Exploring the relationships between strategy, innovation, and management control systems: The roles of social networking, organic, innovative culture, and formal controls. *Journal of Management Accounting Research, 23*(1), 99-128. doi:10.2308/jmar-10069

Chien, S. W., Lin, H. C., & Shih, C. T. (2014). A moderated mediation study: Cohesion linking centrifugal and centripetal forces to ERP implementation performance. *International Journal of Production Economics, 158*(1), 1-8. doi:10.1016/j.ijpe.2014.06.001

Chofreh, A. G., Goni, F. A., Ismail, S., Shaharoun, A. M., Klemeš, J. J., & Zeinalnezhad, M. (2016). A master plan for the implementation of sustainable enterprise resource planning systems (part one): Concept and methodology. *Journal of Cleaner Production, 136*, 176-182. doi:10.1016/j.jclepro.2016.05.140

Chofreh, A. G., Goni, F. A., Shaharoun, A. M., Ismail, S., & Klemeš, J. J. (2014). Sustainable enterprise resource planning: Imperatives and research directions. *Journal of Cleaner Production, 71*, 139-147. doi:10.1016/j.jclepro.2014.01.010

Chow, I. H. S. (2018). The mechanism underlying the empowering leadership-creativity relationship. *Leadership & Organization Development Journal, 39*(2), 202–217. doi:10.1108/lodj-03-2016-0060

Christensen, C. M., & Raynor, M. E. (2003). Why hard-nosed executives should care about management theory. *Harvard Business Review*, 1–9. Retrieved from http://hbr.org/

Chuang, H. M., Lin, C. K., Chen, D. R., Chen, Y. S., & Wang, L. C. (2015). Elucidating the merits of customer relationship management in cloud computing. *Applied Mathematics & Information Sciences, 9*(4), 2001-2013. Retrieved from http://www.naturalspublishing.com/show.asp?JorID=1&pgid=0

Cleland, D. I., & King, W. R. (1983). *Systems analysis and project management*. New York, NY: McGraw-Hill.

Collier-Reed, B. I., Ingerman, Å., & Berglund, A. (2009). Reflections on trustworthiness in phenomenographic research: Recognising purpose, context and change in the process of research. *Education as Change, 13*(2), 339-355. doi:10.1080/16823200903234901

Conceição, S. C. O., & Altman, B. A. (2011). Training and development process and organizational culture change. *Organization Development Journal, 29*(1), 33-43. doi:10.2139/ssrn.2686104

Conteh, N. Y., & Akhtar, M. J. (2015). Implementation challenges of an enterprise system and its advantages over legacy systems. *International Journal on Computer Science and Engineering, 7*(11), 120-128. Retrieved from http://www.enggjournals.com/ijcse/

Cope, D. G. (2014). Methods and meanings: Credibility and trustworthiness of qualitative research. *Oncology Nursing Forum, 41*(1), 89-91. doi:10.1188/14.ONF.89-91

Costa, C. J., Ferreira, E., Bento, F., & Aparicio, M. (2016). Enterprise resource planning adoption and satisfaction determinants. *Computers in Human Behavior, 63*(1), 659–671. doi:10.1016/j.chb.2016.05.090

Coyle, N., & Tickoo, R. (2007). Qualitative research: What this research paradigm has to offer to the understanding of pain. *Pain Medicine, 8*(3), 205–206. doi:10.1111/j.15264637.2007.00303.x

Creswell, J. W. (2007). *Qualitative inquiry and research design: Choosing among five traditions* (2nd ed.). Thousand Oaks, CA: Sage.

Creswell, J. W. (2009). *Research design: Qualitative, quantitative, and mixed methods approaches* (3rd ed.). Thousand Oaks, CA: Sage.

Cronbach, L. J. (1951). Coefficient alpha and the internal structure of tests. *Psychometrika, 16*(3), 297-334. doi:10.1007/bf02310555

Cullinane, S. J., Bosak, J., Flood, P. C., & Demerouti, E. (2017). Job crafting for lean engagement: The interplay of day and job-level characteristics. *European Journal of Work and Organizational Psychology, 26*(4), 541–554. doi:10.1080/1359432x.2017.1320280

Dai, J., & Vasarhelyi, M. A. (2017). Toward blockchain-based accounting and assurance. *Journal of Information Systems, 31*(3), 5-21. doi:10.2308/isys-51804

Dalkey, N., & Helmer, O. (1963). An experimental application of the Delphi method to the use of experts. *Management Science, 9*(3), 458-467. doi:10.1287/mnsc.9.3.458

Dalkey, N., Rourke, D. L., Lewis, R., & Snyder, D. (1972). *Studies in the quality of life: Delphi and decision-making.* Lexington, MA: Lexington Books.

Davis, F. D., Bagozzi, R. P., & Warshaw, P. R. (1989). User acceptance of computer technology: A comparison of two theoretical models, *Management Science, 35* (8): 982–1003. doi:10.1287/mnsc.35.8.982

Day, J., & Bobeva, M. (2005). A generic toolkit for the successful management of Delphi studies. *The Electronic Journal of Business Research Methodology, 3*(2), 103-116. Retrieved from https://doaj.org/toc/1477-7029

Delbecq, A., Gustafson, D., & Van de Ven, A. (1986). *Group techniques for program planning: A guide to nominal group and Delphi processes.* Middleton, WI: Green Briar Press.

DeLone, W. H., & McLean, E. R. (1992). Information systems success: The quest for the dependent variable. *Information Systems Research, 3*(1), 60-95. doi:10.1287/isre.3.1.60

DeLone, W. H., & McLean, E. R. (2003). The DeLone and McLean model of information systems success: A ten-year update. *Journal of management information systems, 19*(4), 9-30. Retrieved from http://www.jstor.org/stable/40398604

Denzin, N. K., & Lincoln, Y. S. (2005). *Qualitative research.* Thousand Oaks, CA: Sage.

Deokar, A. V., & Sarnikar, S. (2016). Understanding process change management in electronic health record implementations. *Information Systems and e-Business Management, 14*(4), 733-766. doi:10.1007/s10257-014-0250-7

De Soete, W. (2016). Towards a multidisciplinary approach on creating value: Sustainability through the supply chain and ERP systems. *Systems, 4*(1), 16-26. doi:10.3390/systems4010016

Diamond, I. R., Grant, R. C., Feldman, B. M., Pencharz, P. B., Ling, S. C., Moore, A. M., & Wales, P. W. (2014). Defining consensus: A systematic review recommends methodologic criteria for reporting of Delphi studies. *Journal of Clinical Epidemiology, 67*(4), 401-409. doi:10.1016/j.jclinepi.2013.12.002

Dixon, R., & Turner, R. (2007). Electronic vs. conventional surveys. *Handbook of Research on Electronic Surveys and Measurements, 7*(3), 105-111. doi:10.4018/978-1-59140-792-8.ch011

Dunn, T. E., Lafferty, C. L., & Alford, K. L. (2012). Global leadership: A new framework for a changing world. *S.A.M. Advanced Management Journal, 77*(2), 4–14. Retrieved from http://samnational.org/

Dwivedi, Y. K., Wastell, D., Laumer, S., Henriksen, H. Z., Myers, M. D., Bunker, D., ... & Srivastava, S. C. (2015). Research on information systems failures and successes: Status update and future directions. *Information Systems Frontiers, 17*(1), 143-157. doi:10.1007/s10796-014-9500-y

Egdair, I. M., Rajemi, M. F., & Nadarajan, S. (2015). Technology factors, ERP system and organization performance in developing countries. *International Journal of Supply Chain Management, 4*(4), 82-89. Retrieved from http://ojs.excelingtech.co.uk/index.php/IJSCM

Eisenhardt, K. M. (1989). Building theories from case study research. *Academy of Management Review, 14*(4), 532-550. doi:10.4135/9781473915480.n52

Elbardan, H., & Kholeif, A. O. (2017). ERP, internal auditing and corporate
governance. *Enterprise Resource Planning, Corporate Governance and
Internal Auditing, 12*(5), 13-54. doi:10.1007/978-3-319-54990-3_2

Elkhani, N., Soltani, S., & Ahmad, M. N. (2014). The effects of transformational
leadership and ERP system self-efficacy on ERP system usage. *Journal of
Enterprise Information Management, 27*(6), 759-785. doi:10.1108/jeim-06-
2013-0031

Elledge, R. O., & McAleer, S. (2015). Planning the content of a brief educational
course in maxillofacial emergencies for staff in accident and emergency
departments: A modified Delphi study. *British Journal of Oral and
Maxillofacial Surgery, 53*(2), 109-113. doi:10.1016/j.bjoms.2014.10.005

Elnasr, E., Sobaih, A., Ritchie, C., & Jones, E. (2012). Consulting the oracle?
Applications of modified Delphi technique to qualitative research in the
hospitality industry. *International Journal of Contemporary Hospitality
Management, 24*(6), 886–906. doi:10.1108/09596111211247227

Etikan, I., Musa, S. A., & Alkassim, R. S. (2016). Comparison of convenience
sampling and purposive sampling. *American Journal of Theoretical and
Applied Statistics, 5*(1), 1-4. doi:10.11648/j.ajtas.20160501.11

Evans, J. R., & Mathur, A. (2005). The value of online surveys. *Internet
Research, 15*(2), 195-219. doi:10.1108/10662240510590360

Fadlalla, A., & Amani, F. (2015). A keyword-based organizing framework for ERP
intellectual contributions. *Journal of Enterprise Information Management,
28*(5), 637-657. doi:10.1108/jeim-09-2014-0090

Fayaz, A., Kamal, Y., Amin, S., & Khan, S. (2017). Critical success factors in
information technology projects. *Management Science Letters, 7*(2), 73-80.
doi:10.5267/j.msl.2016.11.012

Fetters, M. D., Curry, L. A., & Creswell, J. W. (2013). Achieving integration in
mixed methods designs-principles and practices. *Health Services Research,
48*(6), 2134-2156. doi:10.1111/1475-6773.12117

Fink, A., & Kosecoff, J. (1985). *How to conduct surveys: A step-by-step guide.*
London, England: Sage.

Flynn, C. B., Smither, J. W., & Walker, A. G. (2015). Exploring the relationship
between leaders' core self-evaluations and subordinates' perceptions of
servant leadership: A field study. *Journal of Leadership & Organizational
Studies, 23*(3), 260-271. doi:10.1177/1548051815621257

Forcht, K. A., Kieschnick, E., Aldridge, A., & Shorter, J. D. (2007). Implementing
enterprise resource planning (ERP) for strategic competitive advantage.
Journal of Issues in Information Systems, 8(2), 425-429. Retrieved from
http://www.iacis.org/iis/iis.php

Fox, A. R., Gordon, L. K., Heckenlively, J. R., Davis, J. L., Goldstein, D. A.,
Lowder, C. Y., ... & Smith, W. M. (2016). Consensus on the diagnosis and
management of nonparaneoplastic autoimmune retinopathy using a
modified Delphi approach. *American Journal of Ophthalmology, 168*(2),
183-190. doi:10.1016/j.ajo.2016.05.013

Frankfort-Nachmias, C., & Nachmias, D. (2009). *Research methods in the social
sciences* (5th ed.). London, England: Hodder Education.

Fu, H., Chang, T., Ku, C., Chang, T., & Huang, C. (2014). The critical success
factors affecting the adoption of inter-organization systems by SMEs.
Journal of Business & Industrial Marketing, 29(5), 400-416.
doi:10.1108/jbim-04-2012-0070

Fu-Long, J., Lei, C., & Ji-Hong, T. (2017). Applying research On BD-Norlan
model based on big data analysis. *DEStech Transactions on Social
Science, Education and Human Science, 2*(1), 113-118.
doi:10.12783/dtssehs/mess2017/12096

Fusch, P. I., & Ness, L. R. (2015). Are we there yet? Data saturation in qualitative research. *The Qualitative Report, 20*(9), 1408-1416. Retrieved from https://nsuworks.nova.edu/tqr/

Gajic, G., Stankovski, S., Ostojic, G., Tesic, Z., & Miladinovic, L. (2014). Method of evaluating the impact of ERP implementation critical success factors – a case study in oil and gas industries. *Enterprise Information Systems, 8*(1), 84-106. doi:10.1080/17517575.2012.690105

García-Morales, V. J., Jiménez-Barrionuevo, M. M., & Gutiérrez-Gutiérrez, L. (2012). Transformational leadership influence on organizational performance through organizational learning and innovation. *Journal of Business Research, 65*(7), 1040-1050. doi:10.1016/j.jbusres.2011.03.005

García-Sánchez, N., & Pérez-Bernal, L. E. (2007). Determination of critical success factors in implementing an ERP system: A field study in Mexican enterprises. *Information Technology for Development, 13*(3), 293–309. doi:10.1002/itdj.20075

Garg, P., & Agarwal, D. (2014). Critical success factors for ERP implementation in a Fortis hospital: An empirical investigation. *Journal of Enterprise Information Management, 27*(4), 402-423. doi:10.1108/jeim-06-2012-0027

Ghobakhloo, M., Hong, T., Sabouri, M., & Zulkifli, N. (2012). Strategies for successful information technology adoption in small- and medium-sized enterprises. *Information, 3*(3), 36-67. doi:10.3390/info3010036

Ghosh, I., & Biswas, S. (2017). A novel framework of ERP implementation in Indian SMEs: Kernel principal component analysis and intuitionistic Fuzzy TOPSIS driven approach. *Accounting, 3*(2), 107-11. doi:10.5267/j.ac.2016.7.004

Giachetti, R. E. (2016). *Design of enterprise systems: Theory, architecture, and methods.* New York, NY: CRC Press.

Gianni, M., Gotzamani, K., & Tsiotras, G. (2017). Multiple perspectives on integrated management systems and corporate sustainability performance. *Journal of Cleaner Production, 168*(1), 1297-1311. doi:10.1016/j.jclepro.2017.09.061

Gil, L., Ruiz, P., Escrivá, L., Font, G., & Manyes, L. (2017). A decade of Food Safety Management System based on ISO 22000: A global overview. *Toxicología, 34*(1), 84-93. Retrieved from http://www.aetox.es/

Gillespie, N. A., & Mann, L. (2004). Transformational leadership and shared values: the building blocks of trust. *Journal of Managerial Psychology, 19*(6), 588–607. doi:10.1108/02683940410551507

Glaser, B. G., & Strauss, A. L. (2012). *The discovery of grounded theory: Strategies for qualitative research.* New Brunswick, NJ: Aldine Transaction.

Glavas, A., & Mish, J. (2015). Resources and capabilities of triple bottom line firms: Going over old or breaking new ground? *Journal of Business Ethics, 127*(3), 623-642. doi:10.1007/210551-014- 2067-1

Godoe, P., & Johansen, T. S. (2012) Understanding adoption of new technologies: Technology readiness and technology acceptance as an integrated concept. *Journal of European Psychology Students, 3*(1), 38–52. doi:10.5334/jeps.aq

Goodhue, D. L., & Thompson, R. L. (1995). Task-Technology Fit and individual performance. *MIS Quarterly, 19*(2), 213-236. doi:10.2307/249689

Grabski, S. V., Leech, S. A., & Schmidt, P. J. (2011). A review of ERP research: A future agenda for accounting information systems. *Journal of Information Systems, 25*(1), 37-78. doi:10.2308/jis.2011.25.1.37

Grant, A. M. (2012) Leading with meaning: Beneficiary contact, prosocial impact, and the performance effects of transformational leadership. *Academy of Management Journal, 55*(2), 458-476. doi:10.5465/amj.2010.0588

Gray, C. J. (2016). The Delphi technique: Lessons learned from a first-time researcher. *Issues in Information Systems, 17*(4), 91-97. Retrieved from http://www.iacis.org/iis/iis.php

Greenleaf, R. K. (1970). *The servant as leader.* Newton Centre, MA: Robert K. Greenleaf Center.

Greenleaf, R. K. (1977). *Servant leadership: A journey into the nature of legitimate power and greatness.* New York, NY: Paulist Press.

Gromovs, G., & Lammi, K. (2017). Blockchain and internet of things require innovative approach to logistics education. *Transport Problems, 12*(1), 23-34. doi:10.20858/tp.2017.12.se.2

Guest, G., Bunce, A., & Johnson, L. (2006). How many interviews are enough? An experiment with data saturation and variability. *Field Methods, 18*(1), 59-82. doi:10.1177/1525822X05279903

Gupta, H., Aye, K. T., Balakrishnan, R., Rajagopal, S., & Nguwi, Y. Y. (2014). A study of key critical success factors (CSFs) for enterprise resource planning (ERP) systems. *International Journal of Computer and Information Technology, 3*(4), 813-818. Retrieved from https://www.ijcit.com/

Habibi, A., Sarafrazi, A., & Izadyar, S. (2014). Delphi technique theoretical framework in qualitative research. *The International Journal of Engineering and Science, 3*(4), 8-13. Retrieved from http://www.journals.elsevier.com/international-journal-of-engineering-science

Habibzadeh, M., Meshkani, F., & Shoshtari, A. (2016). Identifying and ranking the factors affecting entrepreneurial marketing to facilitate exports. *Management Science Letters, 6*(4), 309-314. doi:10.5267/j.msl.2016.1.010

Haddara, M., & Hetlevik, T. (2016). Investigating the effectiveness of traditional support structures and self-organizing entities within the ERP shakedown phase. *Procedia Computer Science, 100*(1), 507-516. doi:10.1016/j.procs.2016.09.189

Hall, K. K., Baker, T. L., Andrews, M. C., Hunt, T. G., & Rapp, A. A. (2015). The importance of product/service quality for frontline marketing employee outcomes: The moderating effect of leader-member exchange (LMX). *Journal of Marketing Theory and Practice, 24*(1), 23-41. doi:10.1080/10696679.2016.1089762

Hamstra, M. R., Yperen, N. W., Wisse, B., & Sassenberg, K. (2013). Transformational and transactional leadership and followers' achievement goals. *Journal of Business and Psychology, 29*(3), 413-425. doi:10.1007/s10869-013-9322-9

Hannigan, T. J., Cano-Kollmann, M., & Mudambi, R. (2015). Thriving innovation amidst manufacturing decline: The Detroit auto cluster and the resilience of local knowledge production. *Industrial and Corporate Change, 24*(3), 613-634. doi:10.1093/icc/dtv014

Harms, P., & Crede, M. (2010). Emotional intelligence and transformational and transactional leadership: A meta-analysis. *Journal of Leadership & Organizational Studies, 17*(1), 5-17. doi:10.1177/1548051809350894

Harvey, M., & Buckley, M. R. (2002). Assessing the "conventional wisdoms" of management for the 21st century organization. *Organizational Dynamics, 30*(4), 368-378. doi:10.1016/s0090-2616(02)00062-1

Hassan, H., Asad, S., & Hoshino, Y. (2016). Determinants of leadership style in big five personality dimensions. *Universal Journal of Management, 4*(4), 161-179. doi:10.13189/ujm.2016.040402

Hassan, M. K., & Mouakket, S. (2016). ERP and organizational change: A case study examining the implementation of accounting modules. *International Journal of Organizational Analysis, 24*(3), 487-515. doi:10.1108/ijoa-05-2014-0760

Hasson, F., & Keeney, S. (2011). Enhancing rigour in the Delphi technique research. *Technological Forecasting and Social Change, 78*(9), 1695-1704. doi:10.1016/j.techfore.2011.04.005

Hasson, F., Keeney, S., & McKenna, H. (2000). Research guidelines for the Delphi survey technique. *Journal of Advanced Nursing, 32*(4), 1008-1015. doi:10.1046/j.1365-2648.2000.t01-1-01567.x/full

Heitner, K. L., Kahn, A. E., & Sherman, K. C. (2013). Building consensus on defining success of diversity work in organizations. *Consulting Psychology Journal - Practice and Research, 65*(1), *58-73.* doi:10.1037/a0032593

Hicks, R., & Berg, J. A. (2014). Multiple publications from a single study: Ethical dilemmas. *Journal of the American Association of Nurse Practitioners, 26*(5), 233–235. doi:10.1002/2327-6924.12125

Ho, L. T., & Lin, G. C. I. (2004). Critical success factor framework for the implementation of integrated-enterprise systems in the manufacturing environment. *International Journal of Production Research, 42*(17), 3731-3742. doi:10.1080/00207540410001721781

Hofmann, E., & Rüsch, M. (2017). Industry 4.0 and the current status as well as future prospects on logistics. *Computers in Industry, 89*(1), 23-34. doi:10.1016/j.compind.2017.04.002

Hsu, C. C., & Sandford, B. A. (2007). The Delphi technique: Making sense of consensus. *Practical Assessment, Research & Evaluation, 12*(10), 1-8. Retrieved from http://pareonline.net/

Hsu, P. F., Ray, S., & Li-Hsieh, Y. Y. (2014). Examining cloud computing adoption intention, pricing mechanism, and deployment model. *International Journal of Information Management, 34*(4), 474-488. doi:10.1016/j.ijinfomgt.2014.04.006

Hu, J., Pedrycz, W., Wang, G., & Wang, K. (2016). Rough sets in distributed decision information systems. *Knowledge-Based Systems, 94,* 13-22. Retrieved from http://www.journals.elsevier.com/knowledge-based-systems

Huang, J. J. (2016). Resource decision making for vertical and horizontal integration problems in an enterprise. *Journal of the Operational Research Society, 67*(11), 1363-1372. doi:10.1057/jors.2016.24

Hughes, D. L., Dwivedi, Y. K., Rana, N. P., & Simintiras, A. C. (2016). Information systems project failure–analysis of causal links using interpretive structural modelling. *Production Planning & Control, 27*(16), 1313-1333. doi:10.1080/09537287.2016.1217571

Huin, S. (2004). Managing deployment of ERP systems in SMEs using multi-agents. *International Journal of Project Management, 22*(6), 511-517. doi:10.1016/j.ijproman.2003.12.005

Hung, S. Y., Chang, S. I., Hung, H. M., Yen, D. C., & Chou, B. F. (2016). Key success factors of vendor-managed inventory implementation in Taiwan's manufacturing industry. *Journal of Global Information Management, 24*(1), 37-60. doi:10.4018/jgim.2016010103

Iamratanakul, S. F., Badir, Y., Siengthai, S., & Sukhotu, V. (2014). Indicators of best practices in technology product development projects: Prioritizing critical success factors. *International Journal of Managing Projects in Business, 7*(4), 602-623. doi:10.1108/ijmpb-06-2012-0036

Ifinedo, P., & Olsen, D. H. (2014). An empirical research on the impacts of organisational decisions' locus, tasks structure rules, knowledge, and IT function's value on ERP system success. *International Journal of Production Research, 53*(8), 2554-2568. doi:10.1080/00207543.2014.991047

Islam, R., Anis, A., & Abdullah, A. (2015). Identifying and ranking the critical success factors of the challenges in providing quality education by Malaysian private higher learning institutions. *International Journal of the Analytic Hierarchy Process, 7*(1), 3-12. doi:10.13033/ijahp.v7i1.273

Iveroth, E. (2016). Strategies for leading IT-enabled change: Lessons from a global transformation case. *Strategy & Leadership, 44*(2), 39-45. doi:10.1108/sl-06-2015-0050

Jackson, F., Nelson, B. D., & Proudfit, G. H. (2014). In an uncertain world, errors are more aversive: Evidence from the error-related negativity. *Emotion 15(1)*, 12-16. doi:10.1037/emo0000020

Jacobs, F. R., & Weston, F. (2007). Enterprise resource planning (ERP)—A brief history. *Journal of Operations Management, 25*(2), 357-363. doi:10.1016/j.jom.2006.11.005

Jeng, D., & Dunk, N. (2013). Knowledge management enablers and knowledge creation in ERP system success. *International Journal of Electronic Business Management, 11*(8), 49-59. Retrieved from http://ijebm-ojs.ie.nthu.edu.tw/IJEBM_OJS/index.php/IJEBM

Jensen, B. K. (2006). An interview with Jon Piot President and CEO Technisource Management Services Frisco, Texas. *Journal of Information Technology Case and Application Research, 8*(2), 59-61. doi:10.1080/15228053.2006.10856089

Joia, L. A., Macêdo, D. G., & Oliveira, L. G. (2014). Antecedents of resistance to enterprise systems: The IT leadership perspective. *The Journal of High Technology Management Research, 25*(2), 188-200. doi:10.1016/j.hitech.2014.07.008

Joshi, K. D., Kuhn, K. M., & Niederman, F. (2010). Excellence in IT consulting: Integrating multiple stakeholders' perceptions of top performers. *IEEE Transactions on Engineering Management, 57*(4), 589-606. doi:10.1109/tem.2010.2040742

Jrad, R. B. N., & Sundaram, D. (2015, July 6-8). *Challenges of inter-organizational information and middleware system projects: Agility, complexity, success, and failure.* Presented at the 6th International Conference on Information, Intelligence, Systems and Applications (IISA). San Juan, Puerto Rico. doi:10.1109/iisa.2015.7387960

Kaplan, R., & Norton, D. (1996). Using the balanced scorecard as a strategic management system. *Harvard Business Review, 74*(1), 75-85. Retrieved from http://hbr.org/

Kareem, J. (2016). The influence of leadership in building a learning organization. *IUP Journal of Organizational Behavior, 15*(1), 7-18. Retrieved from http://www.iupindia.in/

Kasemsap, K. (2016). Multifaceted applications of data mining, business intelligence, and knowledge management. *International Journal of Social and Organizational Dynamics in IT, 5*(1), 57-69. doi:10.4018/ijsodit.2016010104

Keeney, S., Hasson, F., & McKenna, H. (2006). Consulting the oracle: Ten lessons from using the Delphi technique in nursing research. *Journal of Advanced Nursing, 53*(2), 205-212. doi:10.1111/j.1365-2648.2006.03716.x

Kennedy, K. (2012). A comprehensive global leadership model. *Business Renaissance Quarterly, 7*(1), 75-106. Retrieved from http://www.brqjournal.com/

Kerwin-Boudreau, S., & Butler-Kisber, L. (2016). Deepening understanding in
qualitative inquiry. *The Qualitative Report, 21*(5), 956-971. Retrieved from
https://nsuworks.nova.edu/tqr/

Khan, S., Nicho, M., & Takruri, H. (2016). IT controls in the public cloud: Success
factors for allocation of roles and responsibilities. *Journal of Information
Technology Case and Application Research, 18*(3), 155-180.
doi:10.1080/15228053.2016.1237218

Kim, K., & Altmann, J. (2013). Evolution of software-as-a-service innovation
system through collective intelligence. *International Journal of Cooperative
Information Systems, 22*(3), 1-25. doi:10.1142/S0218843013400066

Krog, C. L., & Govender, K. (2015a, November 12-13). *Servant leadership and
project management: Examining the effects of leadership style on project
success.* Presented at the European Conference on Management,
Leadership & Governance, Lisbon, Portugal. Retrieved from
http://www.academic-conferences.org/conferences/ecmlg/ecmlg-future-and-
past/

Krog, C. L., & Govender, K. (2015b). The relationship between servant
leadership and employee empowerment, commitment, trust and innovative
behaviour: A project management perspective. *SA Journal of Human
Resource Management, 13*(1), 1-12. doi:10.4102/sajhrm.v13i1.712

Kumar, K., & Van Hillegersberg, J. (2000). ERP experiences and evolution.
Communications of the ACM, 43(4), 23-26. Retrieved from
https://cacm.acm.org/

Langley, A. (1999). Strategies for theorizing from process data. *Academy of
Management Review, 24*(4), 691-710. doi:10.2307/259349

Larteb, L., Benhadou, M., Haddout, A., & Nahla, H. (2016). The key to lean
performance: Implementing a daily shop-floor control system using
standardization and visual management. *Journal of Advanced Research in
Management, 7*(1), 34-43. Retrieved from
https://journals.aserspublishing.eu/jarm

Lasi, H., Fettke, P., Kemper, H. G., Feld, T., & Hoffmann, M. (2014). Industry 4.0.
Business & Information Systems Engineering, 6(4), 239-242.
doi:10.1007/s12599-014-0334-4

Latta, G. F. (2009). A process model of organizational change in cultural context
(OC3 model): The impact of organizational culture on leading change.
Journal of Leadership & Organizational Studies, 16(1), 19–37.
doi:10.1177/1548051809334197

Le Pennec, M., & Raufflet, E. (2016). Value creation in inter-organizational
collaboration: An empirical study. *Journal of Business Ethics, 16*(1), 1-18.
doi:10.1007/s10551-015-3012-7

Leshem, S., & Trafford, V. (2007). Overlooking the conceptual framework.
Innovations in Education and Teaching International, 44(1), 93-105.
doi:10.1080/14703290601081407

Leyh, C., & Sander, P. (2015). Critical success factors for ERP system
implementation projects: An update of literature reviews. *Enterprise
Systems: Strategic, Organizational, and Technological Dimensions, 198*(1),
45–67. doi:10.1007/978-3-319-17587-4_3

Li, H. J., Chang, S. I., & Yen, D. C. (2017). Investigating CSFs for the life cycle of
ERP system from the perspective of IT governance. *Computer Standards &
Interfaces, 50*(1), 269-279. doi:10.1016/j.csi.2016.10.013

Li, Z., Wang, W. M., Liu, G., Liu, L., He, J., & Huang, G. Q. (2018). Toward open
manufacturing: A cross-enterprises knowledge and services exchange
framework based on blockchain and edge computing. *Industrial
Management & Data Systems, 118*(1), 303-320. doi:10.1108/IMDS-04-

2017-0142

Lin, C., Ma, Z., & Lin, R. C. (2011). Re-examining the critical success factors of e-learning from the EU perspective. *International Journal of Management in Education, 5*(1), 44-62. doi:10.1504/IJMIE.2011.037754

Lin, H. (2010). An investigation into the effects of IS quality and top management support of ERP system usage. *Total Quality Management & Business Excellence, 21*(3), 335-349. doi:10.1080/14783360903561761

Lincoln, Y., & Guba, E. (1985). *Naturalistic inquiry.* Newbury Park, CA: Sage.

Linstone, H. A., & Turoff, M. (2002). *The Delphi method: Techniques and applications.* Reading, MA: Addison-Wesley.

Lohuis, A. M., van Vuuren, M., & Bohlmeijer, E. (2013). Context-specific definitions of organizational concepts: Defining 'team effectiveness' with use of the Delphi technique. *Journal of Management and Organization, 19*(6), 706-720. doi:10.1017/jmo.2014.10

Loo, R. (2002). The Delphi method: A powerful tool for strategic management. *Policing: An International Journal of Police Strategies & Management, 25*(4), 762-769. doi:10.1108/13639510210450677

Loonam, J., Kumar, V., Mitra, A., & Abd Razak, A. (2018). Critical success factors for the implementation of enterprise systems: A literature review. *Strategic Change, 27*(3), 185-194. doi:10.1002/jsc.2194

Love, P. E., Matthews, J., Simpson, I., Hill, A., & Olatunji, O. A. (2014). A benefits realization management building information modeling framework for asset owners. *Automation in Construction, 37*(1), 1-10. doi:10.1016/j.autcon.2013.09.007

Low, S. A., & Brown, J. P. (2017). Manufacturing plant survival in a period of decline. *Growth and Change, 48*(3), 297-312. doi:10.1111/grow.12171

Lozano, R. (2014). Creativity and organizational learning as means to foster sustainability. *Sustainable Development, 22*(3), 205-216. doi:10.1002/sd.540

Ludlow, A., & Blackham, A. (2015). *New frontiers in empirical labour law research.* Portland, OR: Bloomsbury Publishing.

Ludwig, B. (1997). Predicting the future: Have you considered using the Delphi methodology? *Journal of Extension, 35*(5), 1-4. Retrieved from http://www.joe.org/

Maas, J., Fenema, P. C., & Soeters, J. (2014). ERP system usage: The role of control and empowerment. *New Technology, Work and Employment, 29*(1), 88-103. doi:10.1111/ntwe.12021

Maditinos, D., Chatzoudes, D., & Tsairidis, C. (2012). Factors affecting ERP system implementation effectiveness. *Journal of Enterprise Information Management, 25*(1), 60-78. doi:10.1108/17410391211192161

Mahdavian, M., Wingreen, S. C., & Ghlichlee, B. (2016). The influence of key users' skills on ERP success. *Journal of Information Technology Management, 27*(2), 48-64. doi:10.1007/s00170-013-5144-1

Malaurent, J., & Avison, D. (2015). From an apparent failure to a success story: ERP in China-post implementation. *International Journal of Information Management, 35*(5), 643-646. doi:10.1016/j.ijinfomgt.2015.06.004

Markus, M. L., Axline, S., Petrie, D., & Tanis, S. C. (2000). Learning from adopters' experiences with ERP: Problems encountered and success achieved. *Journal of Information Technology, 15*(4), 245-265. doi:10.1080/02683960010008944

Marques, M., Agostinho, C., Zacharewicz, G., & Jardim-Gonçalves, R. (2017). Decentralized decision support for intelligent manufacturing in Industry 4.0. *Journal of Ambient Intelligence and Smart Environments, 9*(3), 299-313. doi.org/10.3233/ais-170436

Martin, C. C. (1976). *Project management: How to make it work.* New York, NY:
Amacom.

May, J., Dhillon, G., & Caldeira, M. (2013). Defining value-based objectives for
ERP systems planning. *Decision Support Systems, 55*(1), 98-109.
doi:10.1016/j.dss.2012.12.036

Mayeh, M., Ramayah, T., & Mishra, A. (2016). The role of absorptive capacity,
communication and trust in ERP adoption. *Journal of Systems and
Software, 119*(1), 58-69. doi:10.1016/j.jss.2016.05.025

McMillan, S. S., King, M., & Tully, M. P. (2016). How to use the nominal group
and Delphi techniques. *International Journal of Clinical Pharmacy, 38*(3),
655-662. doi:10.1007/s11096-016-0257-x

Minner, W. (2015). Leading global organizations. *Journal of Management Policy
and Practice, 16*(2), 122-126. Retrieved from http://www.na-
businesspress.com/jmppopen.html

Mitchell, V. W. (1991). The Delphi technique: An exposition and application.
Technology Analysis & Strategic Management, 3(4), 333-358.
doi:10.1080/09537329108524065

Mitra, P., & Mishra, S. (2016). Behavioral aspects of ERP implementation: A
conceptual review. *Interdisciplinary Journal of Information, Knowledge, and
Management, 11*(1), 17-30. Retrieved from
http://www.informingscience.org/Journals/IJIKM/

Mittal, S. (2016). Effects of transformational leadership on turnover intentions in
IT SMEs. *International Journal of Manpower, 37*(8), 1322-1346.
doi:10.1108/IJM-10-2014-0202

Mo, J., & He, W. (2015). The organizational change dilemma of ERP
implementation in a small manufacturing company. *Journal of Business
Case Studies, 11*(3), 95. doi:10.19030/jbcs.v11i3.9273

Mokkink, L. B., Terwee, C. B., Patrick, D. L., Alonso, J., Stratford, P. W., Knol, D.
L., ... & De Vet, H. C. (2010). The COSMIN checklist for assessing the
methodological quality of studies on measurement properties of health
status measurement instruments: An international Delphi study. *Quality of
Life Research, 19*(4), 539-549. doi:10.1007/s11136-010-9606-8

Moustakas, C. (1994). *Phenomenological research methods.* Thousand Oaks,
CA: Sage.

Mudzana, T., & Maharaj, M. (2015). Measuring the success of business-
intelligence systems in South Africa: An empirical investigation applying the
DeLone and McLean model. *South African Journal of Information
Management, 17*(1), 1-7. doi:10.4102/sajim.v17i1.646

Müller, R., & Turner, R. (2007). The influence of project managers on project
success criteria and project success by type of project. *European
Management Journal, 25*(4), 298-309. doi:10.1016/j.emj.2007.06.003

Mwayongo, S. J., & Omar, N. (2017). Effects of e-inventory management on
procurement processes of government corporations in Kenya. *Imperial
Journal of Interdisciplinary Research, 3*(11), 345-369. Retrieved from
https://www.onlinejournal.in/

Ndalila, P., Mjema, E. A., Kundi, B. A., & Kerefu, L. J. (2015). Human resource
competency structure for organizational innovation leadership in
engineering-based research and development institutions in Tanzania.
Journal of Multidisciplinary Engineering Science and Technology, 2(7),
1695-1702. Retrieved from http://www.jmest.org/

Newman, I., & Covrig, D. M. (2013). Building consistency between title, problem
statement, purpose, & research questions to improve the quality of research
plans and reports. *New Horizons in Adult Education & Human Resource
Development, 25*(1), 70-79. doi:10.1002/nha.20009

Ngai, E. W., Cheng, T. C. E., & Ho, S. S. M. (2004). Critical success factors of web-based supply-chain management systems: An exploratory study. *Production Planning & Control, 15*(6), 622-630. doi:10.1080/09537280412331283928

Ngai, E. W., Law, C. C., & Wat, F. K. (2008). Examining the critical success factors in the adoption of enterprise resource planning. *Computers in Industry, 59*(6), 548-564. doi:10.1016/j.compind.2007.12.001

Nunnally, J. C. (1967). *Psychometric theory*. New York, NY: McGraw Hill.

Okoli, C., & Pawlowski, S. D. (2004). The Delphi method as a research tool: An example, design considerations and applications. *Information & Management, 42*(1), 15-29. doi:10.1016/j.im.2003.11.002

Oppenheim, A. N. (1992). *Questionnaire, design, interviewing and attitude measurement*. London, England: Pinter Publishing Limited.

Orlikowski, W. J. (1993) CASE tools as organizational change: Investigating incremental and radical changes in systems development. *MIS Quarterly, 17*(1), 309– 340. doi:10.4135/9781849209687.n11

Orouji, M. (2016). Critical success factors in project management. *Journal of Project Management, 1*(1), 35-40. Retrieved from http://www.growingscience.com

Orr, L. M., & Orr, D. J. (2013). *When to hire or not hire a consultant: Getting your money's worth from consulting relationships*. Berkeley, CA: Apress Publishing.

Orte, C., Ballester, L., Amer, J., & Vives, M. (2014). Assessing the role of facilitators inevidence-based family-centric prevention programs via Delphi technique. *Families in Society: The Journal of Contemporary Social Services, 95*(4), 236-244. doi:10.1606/1044-3894.2014.95.30

Palanisamy, R., Verville, J., & Taskin, N. (2015). The critical success factors (CSFs) for enterprise software contract negotiations. *Journal of Enterprise Information Management, 28*(1), 34-59. doi:10.1108/jeim-12-2013-0083

Paoloni, M., Bernetti, A., Brignoli, O., Coclite, D., Fraioli, A., Masiero, S., ... & Viora, U. (2017). Appropriateness and efficacy of spa therapy for musculoskeletal disorders. A Delphi method consensus initiative among experts in Italy. *Ann Ist Super Sanita, 53*(1), 70-76. Retrieved from https://www.ncbi.nlm.nih.gov/labs/journals/ann-ist-super-sanita/

Peng, G. C. A., & Nunes, M. B. (2013). Establishing and verifying a risk ontology for surfacing ERP post-implementation risks. *Enterprise Resource Planning: Concepts, Methodologies, Tools, and Applications: Concepts, Methodologies, Tools, and Applications, 4*(1), 450–474. doi:10.4018/978-1-4666-4153-2.ch025

Petter, S., & McLean, E. R. (2009). A meta-analytic assessment of the DeLone and McLean IS success model: An examination of IS success at the individual level. *Information & Management, 46*(3), 159-166. doi:10.1016/j.im.2008.12.006

Pishdad, A., Koronios, A., Reich, B. H., & Geursen, G. (2014). ERP institutionalisation- A quantitative data analysis using the integrative framework of IS theories. *Journal of Information Systems, 18*(3), 347-369. doi:10.3127/ajis.v18i3.1089

Polkinghorne, D. E. (1989). Phenomenological research methods. *Existential-Phenomenological Perspectives in Psychology, 4(1)*, 41-60. doi:10.1007/978-1-4615-6989-3_3

Porter, M. E. (2011). *Competitive advantage of nations: Creating and sustaining superior performance*. New York, NY: The Free Press.

Powell, C. (2003). The Delphi technique: Myths and realities. *Journal of Advanced Nursing, 41*(4), 376-382. doi:10.1046/j.1365-2648.2003.02537.x

Qin, S., & Kai, C. (2016). Special issue on future digital design and manufacturing: Embracing industry 4.0 and beyond. *Chinese Journal of Mechanical Engineering, 29*(6), 1045-1045. doi:10.3901/cjme.2016.0909.110

Rai, A., Lang, S. S., & Welker, R. B. (2002). Assessing the validity of IS success models: An empirical test and theoretical analysis. *Information Systems Research, 13*(1), 50–69. doi:10.1287/isre.13.1.50.96

Ram, J., & Corkindale, D. (2014). How "critical" are the critical success factors (CSFs)? Examining the role of CSFs for ERP. *Business Process Management Journal, 20*(1), 151-174. doi:10.1108/BPMJ-11-2012-0127

Ram, J., Wu, M. L., & Tagg, R. (2014). Competitive advantage from ERP projects: Examining the role of key implementation drivers. *International Journal of Project Management, 32*(4), 663-675. doi:10.1109/EMR.2014.6966923

Ranjan, S., Jha, V. K., & Pal, P. (2016). A strategic and sustainable multi-criteria decision-making framework for ERP selection in OEM. *International Journal of Applied Engineering Research, 11*(3), 1916-1926. Retrieved from https://www.ripublication.com/ijaer.htm

Rashid, A., Masood, T., Erkoyuncu, J. A., Tjahjono, B., Khan, N., & Shami, M. U. D. (2018). Enterprise systems' life cycle in pursuit of resilient smart factory for emerging aircraft industry: A synthesis of critical success factors' (CSFs), theory, knowledge gaps, and implications. *Enterprise Information Systems, 12*(2), 96-136. doi:10.1080/17517575.2016.1258087

Ravasan, A., & Mansouri, T. (2016). A dynamic ERP critical failure factors modelling with FCM throughout project lifecycle phases. *Production Planning & Control, 27*(2), 65-82. doi:10.1080/09537287.2015.1064551

Ravitch, S. M., & Carl, N. M. (2016). Qualitative research: Bridging the conceptual, theoretical, and methodological. Thousand Oaks, CA: Sage.

Razzhivina, M. A., Yakimovich, B. A., & Korshunov, A. I. (2015). Application of information technologies and principles of lean production for efficiency improvement of machine building enterprises. *Pollack Periodica, 10*(2), 17-23. doi:10.1556/606.2015.10.2.2

Remus, U. (2007). Critical success factors for implementing enterprise portals: A comparison with ERP implementations. *Business Process Management Journal, 13*(4), 538-552. doi:10.1108/14637150710763568

Remus, U., & Wiener, M. (2010). A multi-method, holistic strategy for researching critical success factors in IT projects. *Information Systems Journal, 20*(1), 25-52. doi:10.1111/j.1365-2575.2008.00324.x

Rezania, D., & Ouedraogo, N. (2013). Organization development through ad hoc problem solving. *International Journal of Managing Projects in Business, 7*(1), 23-42. doi:10.1108/ijmpb-11-2012-0067

Rockart, J. F. (1979). Chief executives define their own data needs. *Harvard Business Review, 57*(2), 81-93. Retrieved from https://www.ncbi.nlm.nih.gov/

Romano, A. R. (2010). Malleable Delphi: Delphi research technique, its evolution, and business application. *International Review of Business Research Papers, 6*(5), 235-243. Retrieved from http://www.irbrp.com/

Rubin, I. M., & Seeling, W. (1967). Experience as a factor in the selection and performance of project managers. *IEEE Transactions on Engineering Management, 14*(3), 131–135. doi:10.1109/tem.1967.6448338

Saade, R. G., & Nijher, H. (2016). Critical success factors in enterprise resource planning implementation. *Journal of Enterprise Information Management, 29*(1), 72-96. doi:10.1108/jeim-03-2014-0028

Salimi, F., Dankbaar, B., & Davidrajuh, R. (2015). A comprehensive study on the differences between MRP and ERP implementation. *Communications of the IIMA, 6*(1), 83-93. Retrieved from http://www.iima.org/

San-Jose, L., & Retolaza, J. L. (2016). Is the Delphi method valid for business ethics? A survey analysis. *European Journal of Futures Research, 4*(1), 19-34. doi:10.1007/s40309-016-0109-x

Sayles, L. R., & Chandler, M. K. (1971). *Managing large systems: Organizations in the future.* New York, NY: Harper & Row.

Scandura, T. A., & Pellegrini, E. K. (2008). Trust and leader-member exchange: A closer look at relational vulnerability. *Journal of Leadership & Organizational Studies, 15*(2), 101-110. doi:10.1177/1548051808320986

Scholtz, B., Calitz, A., & Cilliers, C. (2013). Usability evaluation of a medium-sized ERP system in higher education. *Electronic Journal of Information Systems Evaluation, 16*(2), 86-99. Retrieved from http://www.ejise.com

Schönberger, M., & Čirjevskis, A. (2017). Successful IT/IS projects in healthcare: Evaluation of critical success factors. *Journal of E-health Management, 17*(2), 1-18. doi:10.5171/2017.956068

Seddon, P. B. (1997). A respecification and extension of the DeLone and McLean model of IS success. *Information Systems Research, 8*(3), 240-253. doi:10.1287/isre.8.3.240

Seddon, P. B., & Kiew, M. (1996). A partial test and development of DeLone and McLean's model of IS Success. *Australasian Journal of Information Systems, 4*(1), 90-109. doi:10.3127/ajis.v4i1.379

Senge, P. M. (1990). The fifth discipline: The art and practice of the learning organization. New York, NY: Doubleday.

Seth, M., Goyal, D. P., & Kiran, R. (2017). Diminution of impediments in implementation of supply chain management information system for enhancing its effectiveness in Indian automobile industry. *Journal of Global Information Management, 25*(3), 1-20. doi:10.4018/jgim.2017070101

Shao, Z., Feng, Y., & Hu, Q. (2016). Effectiveness of top management support in enterprise systems success: A contingency perspective of fit between leadership style and system life-cycle. *European Journal of Information Systems, 25*(2), 131-153. doi:10.1057/ejis.2015.6

Shao, Z., Wang, T., & Feng, Y. (2015). Impact of organizational culture and computer self-efficacy on knowledge sharing. *Industrial Management & Data Systems, 115*(4), 590-611. doi:10.1108/IMDS-12-2014-037

Sharma, V., Dixit, A. R., & Qadri, M. A. (2015). Impact of lean practices on performance measures in context to Indian machine tool industry. *Journal of Manufacturing Technology Management, 26*(8), 1218-1242. doi:10.1108/JMTM-11-2014-0118

Shen, Y., Chen, P., & Wang, C. (2016). A study of enterprise resource planning (ERP) system performance measurement using the quantitative balanced scorecard approach. *Computers in Industry, 75*(1), 127-139. doi:10.1016/j.compind.2015.05.006

Shenton, A. K. (2004). Strategies for ensuring trustworthiness in qualitative research projects. *Education for Information, 22*(2), 63-75. doi:10.3233/efi-2004-22201

Shiri, S., Anvari, A., & Soltani, H. (2014). As assessment of readiness factors for implementing ERP based on agility. *International Journal of Management, Accounting & Economics, 1*(3), 229-246. Retrieved from http://www.ijmae.com/

Sikdar, A., & Payyazhi, J. (2014). A process model of managing organizational change during business process redesign. *Business Process Management Journal, 20*(6), 971-998. doi:10.1108/bpmj-02-2013-0020

Singh, A., & Nagpal, S. (2014). Implementation of ERP in cloud computing.

International Journal of Scientific & Technology Research, 3(10), 100-103.
Retrieved from www.ijstr.org

Siricha, P. S., & Theuri, F. S. (2016). The effects of electronic procurement on organizational performance in Kenya ports authority. *Imperial Journal of Interdisciplinary Research*, 2(11), 1761-1783. Retrieved from https://www.onlinejournal.in/

Skulmoski, G. J., Hartman, F. T., & Krahn, J. (2010). The Delphi method for graduate research. *Journal of Information Technology Education*, 6(1), 1-21. Retrieved from http://ijiet.org/

Smith, R. E., Bonacina, C., Kearney, P., & Merlat, W. (2000). Embodiment of evolutionary computation in general agents. *Evolutionary Computation*, 8(4), 475-493. doi:10.1162/106365600568266

Soler, İ. S., Feliks, J., & Ömürgönülşen, M. (2016). The measurement of the perception of the relationship between selection criteria and critical success factors of enterprise resource planning. *International Journal of Business and Social Science*, 7(5), 36-47. doi:10.30845/ijbss

Solutions, P. C. (2016). 2016 report on ERP systems and enterprise software. 1-32. Retrieved from http://panorama-consulting.com/resource-center/2016-erp-report/

Stanciu, V., & Tinca, A. (2013). ERP solutions between success and failure. *Accounting & Management Information Systems*, 12(4), 626-649. Retrieved from http://jamis.ase.ro/

Steurer, J. (2011). The Delphi method: An efficient procedure to generate knowledge. *Skeletal Radiology*, 40(8), 959-961. doi:10.1007/s00256-011-1145-z

Stocker, A., & Müller, J. (2016). Exploring use and benefit of corporate social software: Measuring success in the Siemens case. *Journal of Systems and Information Technology*, 18(3), 277-296. doi:10.1108/jsit-03-2016-0021

Sudhaman, P., & Thangavel, C. (2015). Efficiency analysis of ERP projects – software quality perspective. *International Journal of Project Management*, 33(4). 961-970. doi:10.1016/j.ijproman.2014.10.011

Sun, H., Ni, W., & Lam, R. (2015). A step-by-step performance assessment and improvement method for ERP implementation: Action case studies in Chinese companies. *Computers in Industry*, 68(1), 40-52. doi:10.1016/j.compind.2014.12.005

Taraba, T., Mikusz, M., & Herzwurm, G. (2014, June 16-18). *A comparative perspective between investors and businesses regarding success factors of e-ventures at an early-stage*. Presented at the International Conference of Software Business. Paphos, Cyprus. doi:10.1007/978-3-319-08738-2

Tarhini, A., Ammar, H., & Tarhini, T. (2015). Analysis of the critical success factors for enterprise resource planning implementation from stakeholders' perspective: A systematic review. *International Business Research*, 8(4), 25-40. doi:10.5539/ibr.v8n4p25

Tatari, O., Castro-Lacouture, D., & Skibniewski, M. J. (2007). Current state of construction enterprise information systems: Survey research. *Construction Innovation*, 7(4), 310–319. doi:10.1108/14714170710780075

Tavakol, M., & Dennick, R. (2011). Making sense of Cronbach's alpha. *International Journal of Medical Education*, 2(1), 53-55. doi:10.5116/ijme.4dfb.8dfd

Thakur, M. A. (2016). Enterprise resource planning (ERP) implementation in technical educational institutes: Prospects and challenges. *International Journal of Multifaceted and Multilingual Studies*, 3(2), 1-5. Retrieved from www.ijmms.in

Thomas, E., & Magilvy, J. K. (2011). Qualitative rigor or research validity in

qualitative research. *Journal for Specialists in Pediatric Nursing, 16*(2), 151-
155. doi:10.1111/j.1744-6155.2011.00283.x

Tripathi, S., & Jigeesh, N. (2015). Task-technology fit (TTF) model to evaluate
adoption of cloud computing: a multi-case study. *International Journal of
Applied Engineering Research, 10*(3), 9185-9200. Retrieved from
http://www.ripublication.com

Tsai, M., Li, E., Lee, K., & Tung, W. (2011). Beyond ERP implementation: The
moderating effect of knowledge management on business performance.
Total Quality Management & Business Excellence, 22(2), 131-144.
doi:10.1080/14783363.2010.529638

Tsai, W. H., Lin, T. W., Chen, S. P., & Hung, S. J. (2007). Users' service quality
satisfaction and performance improvement of ERP consultant selections.
International Journal of Business and Systems Research, 1(3), 280-301.
doi:10.1504/ijbsr.2007.015830

Turner, J. (2014). Grounded theory building performance for the workplace.
Performance Improvement, 53(3), 31-38. doi:10.1002/pfi.21401

Turner, N., Kutsch, E., & Leybourne, S. A. (2016). Rethinking project reliability
using the ambidexterity and mindfulness perspectives. *International Journal
of Managing Projects in Business, 9*(4), 845-864. doi:10.1108/ijmpb-08-
2015-0074

Ulhøi, J. P., & Müller, S. (2014). Mapping the landscape of shared leadership: A
review and synthesis. *International Journal of Leadership Studies, 8*(2), 66-
87. Retrieved from
https://www.regent.edu/acad/global/publications/ijls/new/home.htm

United States Department of Labor, Bureau of Labor Statistics. (2019, January).
Industries at a Glance. Manufacturing: NAICS 31-33. Retrieved from
http://www.bls.gov/iag/tgs/iag31-33.htm

Upadhyay, P., Basu, R., Adhikary, R., & Dan, P. K. (2010). A comparative study
of issues affecting ERP implementation in large scale and small medium
scale enterprises in India: A Pareto approach. *International Journal of
Computer Applications, 8*(3), 23-28. doi:10.5120/1192-1670

Upton, D., & Upton, P. (2006). Development of an evidence-based practice
questionnaire for nurses. *Journal of Advanced Nursing, 53*(4), 454-458.
doi:10.1111/j.1365-2648.2006.03739.x

Uwizeyemungu, S., & Raymond, L. (2009). Exploring an alternative method of
evaluating the effects of ERP: A multiple case study. *Journal of Information
Technology, 24*(3), 251–268. doi:10.1057/jit.2008.20

Venkatesh, V., Morris, M. G., Davis, G. B., & Davis, F. D. (2003). User
acceptance of information technology: Toward a unified view. *MIS
Quarterly, 27*(3), 425-478. doi:10.2307/30036540

Venkatraman, S., & Fahd, K. (2016). Challenges and success factors of ERP
systems in Australian SMEs. *Systems, 4*(2), 1-18.
doi:10.3390/systems4020020

Verdouw, C., Robbemond, R., & Wolfert, J. (2015). ERP in agriculture: Lessons
learned from the Dutch horticulture. *Computers and Electronics in
Agriculture, 114*(1), 125-133. doi:10.1016/j.compag.2015.04.002

von der Gracht, H. A., & Darkow, I. L. (2013). The future role of logistics for
global wealth–scenarios and discontinuities until 2025. *Foresight, 15*(5),
405-419. doi:10.1108/fs-05-2012-0031

Vrasidas, C., & Zembylas, M. (2004). Online professional development: Lessons
from the field. *Education+Training, 46*(6/7), 326-334.
doi:10.1108/00400910410555231

Wang, J., Wu, P., Wang, X., & Shou, W. (2017). The outlook of blockchain
technology for construction engineering management. *Frontiers of*

Engineering Management, 4(1), 67-75. doi:10.15302/J-FEM-2017006

Wang, P., & Zhu, W. (2010). Mediating role of creative identity in the influence of transformational leadership on creativity: Is there a multilevel effect? Journal of Leadership & Organizational Studies, 18(1), 25- 39. doi:10.1177/1548051810368549

Wijkstra, P. J., TenVergert, E. M., Van Altena, R., Otten, V., Postma, D. S., Kraan, J., & Koeter, G. H. (1994). Reliability and validity of the Chronic Respiratory Questionnaire (CRQ). Thorax, 49(5), 465-467. Retrieved from http://thorax.bmj.com/

Xie, Y., Allen, C. J., & Ali, M. (2014). An integrated decision support system for ERP implementation in small and medium sized enterprises. Journal of Enterprise Information Management, 27(4), 358-384. doi:10.1108/JEIM-10-2012-0077

Yassien, E. (2017). Software projects success by objectives. Journal of Management Research, 10(1), 46-57. doi:10.5296/jmr.v10i1.10149

Yurtseven, M. K., & Buchanan, W. W. (2016). Complexity decision making and general systems theory: An educational perspective. Sociology, 6(2), 77-95. doi:10.17265/2159-5526/2016.02.001

Zach, O., & Munkvold, B. E. (2012). Identifying reasons for ERP system customization in SMEs: A multiple case study. Journal of Enterprise Information Management, 25(5), 462-478. doi:10.1108/17410391211265142

Zeng, Y. R., Wang, L., & Xu, X. H. (2015). An integrated model to select an ERP system for Chinese small and medium-sized enterprise under uncertainty. Technological and Economic Development of Economy, 23(1), 38–58. doi:10.3846/20294913.2015.1072748

Zha, Q., & Tu, D. (2016). Doing mixed methods research in comparative education: Some reflections on the fit and a survey of the literature. International Perspectives on Education & Society, 28(1), 165-191. doi:10.1108/S1479-367920150000028014

Zhang, J., Schmidt, K., & Li, H. (2016). An integrated diagnostic framework to manage organization sustainable growth: An empirical case. Sustainability, 8(4), 301-326. doi:10.3390/su8040301

Zigurs, I., & Buckland, B. K. (1998). A theory of task/technology fit and group support systems effectiveness. MIS Quarterly, 22(3), 313-334. doi:10.2307/249668

Zouine, A., & Fenies, P. (2015). A new evaluation model of ERP system success. Journal of Intelligence Studies in Business, 5(1), 18-39. Retrieved from http://ojs.hh.se/index.php/JISIB

Zughoul, B., Al-Refai, M., & El-Omari, N. (2016). Evolution characteristics of ERP systems that distinct from traditional SDLCs. Evolution, 5(7), 87-91. doi:10.17148/ijarcce.2016.5718

Zvezdov, D., & Hack, S. (2016). Carbon footprinting of large product portfolios. Extending the use of enterprise resource planning systems to carbon information management. Journal of Cleaner Production, 135(1), 1267-1275. doi:10.1016/j.jclepro.2016.06.070

APPENDICES

Appendix A: Permission for Research Within a LinkedIn Group

Dear LinkedIn Moderator,

I am a doctoral student conducting a research study among ERP manufacturing consultants on the critical success factors in ERP implementations in small- and medium-sized enterprises in the United States. I would like to ask your permission to post a message to your group to invite participants to join my study for each round of the surveys. If you agree, could you please acknowledge this message? Also, if you agree, I will provide you with invitations that will include information about the research purpose as well as the SurveyMonkey link to access the survey. Thank you for your consideration, and I look forward to your response in building on the ERP body of knowledge.

Regards, Justin Goldston, CSCP, LSSGB, PSM, PLS

Appendix B: LinkedIn Group Messaging

Round 1 LinkedIn Group Messaging

Dear ERP manufacturing consultant,

You have been invited to take part in a research study about critical success factors in Enterprise Resource Planning (ERP) implementations in the United States. This study is being conducted by Justin Goldston, who is a doctoral student at Walden University. You may already know the researcher as a Senior Management Consultant, but this study is separate from that role.

The purpose of this Delphi study is to identify a consensus among a panel of ERP manufacturing consultants as to the desirability and feasibility of critical success factors in ERP implementations in the United States. The study will involve at least three rounds of data collection and analysis.

To be eligible for the study, you should meet the following criteria:

a) have at least five years of experience implementing ERP applications
b) perform ERP implementations in the United States
c) perform ERP implementations in the industrial or manufacturing sector
d) perform ERP implementations for small- and medium-sized enterprises (firms that employ fewer than 500 employees).

If you would like to participate in the study, please select the following link:

https://www.SurveyMonkey/r/erpcriticalsuccessfactors1

You may ask any questions you have now by contacting the researcher via ███████████████████████ or █████████████.

Thank you for your consideration, and I look forward to your response in building on the ERP body of knowledge.

(Private information, e.g., phone numbers and email addresses, were redacted to retain privacy of the noted entities.)

Appendix C: Survey Screening Questions

*1. Do you have at least five years of experience
implementing ERP applications?

☐ Yes
☐ No

*2. Have you performed ERP implementations in the United
States?

☐ Yes
☐ No

*3. Have you performed ERP implementations in the
industrial or manufacturing sector?

☐ Yes
☐ No

*4. Have you performed ERP implementations for small- and
medium-sized enterprises (firms that employ fewer than 500
employees)?

☐ Yes
☐ No

Appendix D: Round 1 Survey Questions

Critical Success Factors in Enterprise Resource Planning Implementation in U.S. Manufacturing

Please rate each critical success factor as it pertains to the desirability of its application in ERP implementations using the following scale.

The definition of each point on the scale is as follows:

1-Highly undesirable: Will have a major negative impact to the implementation.

2-Undesirable: Will have a negative impact to the implementation with little positive to no positive effect.

3-Neutral: Will have no impact on the implementation.

4-Desirable: Will have a minimal positive impact to the implementation with little negative effect.

5-Highly desirable: Will have a positive impact to the implementation with no negative effect.

1. Cultural change readiness (CCR) - Cultural and structural changes; cultural readiness; social aspects	1	2	3	4	5
2. Top management support and commitment (TMSC) - Company-wide support; empowered decision makers; stakeholder commitment; supportive IT infrastructure; top management support	1	2	3	4	5
3. Knowledge capacity production network (KCPN) - Network relationships; knowledge capacity; detailed planning; client consultation	1	2	3	4	5
4. Minimum customization (MC) - Minimum customization	1	2	3	4	5
5. Legacy systems support (LSS) - Legacy systems	1	2	3	4	5
6. ERP fit with the organization (EFO) - ERP package selection; alignment of ERP with business requirement	1	2	3	4	5
7. Local vendors partnership (LVP) - Software vendor; partnership with local vendors	1	2	3	4	5
8. Detailed cost (DC) - Cost of ERP implementation	1	2	3	4	5
9. Business process re-engineering (BPR) - Business process re-engineering; country specific business process; consultant's expertise	1	2	3	4	5

10. Quality management (QM) - Data integration; data accuracy; quality management	1	2	3	4	5
11. Risk management (RM) - Risk management	1	2	3	4	5
12. Detailed data migration plan (DMP) - Data migration plan	1	2	3	4	5
13. Measurable goals (MG) - Comprehensiveness of implementation strategy; clear and measurable goals; coordinated analysis	1	2	3	4	5
14. Small internal team of best employees (STBE) - Cross-functional employees in the team; best people in the team; multi-functional project team; ERP teamwork; multi-functional project team; small internal team	1	2	3	4	5
15. Open and transparent communication (OTC) - Interdepartmental communication; open information and communication policy	1	2	3	4	5
16. Base point analysis (BPA) - Process discipline; benchmarking	1	2	3	4	5
17. Morale maintenance (MM) - Morale of the implementation team; celebrating small wins	1	2	3	4	5
18. Contingency plans (CP) - Co-ordinated analysis; contingency plans	1	2	3	4	5

19. ERP success documentation (ESD) - Document ERP success	1	2	3	4	5
20. User feedback usage (UFU) - User feedback; harmonized modeling; optimization opportunities	1	2	3	4	5
21. Maximum potential usage (MPU) - Effective use of ERP application	1	2	3	4	5
22. Results measurement (RM) - Results measurement; focused performance measures; performance evaluation; post-implementation audit	1	2	3	4	5

Demographic Questions

23. Please state your age range:

☐ 21 and under
☐ 22 to 34
☐ 35 to 44
☐ 45 to 54
☐ 55 to 64
☐ 65 and over

24. Please indicate your gender:

    (open text box)

25. What is the highest level of education completed?

☐ High School
☐ Bachelor's Degree
☐ Master's Degree
☐ Doctoral Degree

26. Years of experience implementing ERP applications in small- and medium-sized manufacturing environments?

☐ 5 to 10 years
☐ 11 to 15 years
☐ 16 to 20 years
☐ 21 years or more

27. Number of implementations completed in small- and medium-sized manufacturing environments?

☐ 1 to 5
☐ 6 to 10
☐ 11 to 15
☐ 16 to 20
☐ 20 or more

28. Geographic region?

☐ Northeast
☐ Midwest
☐ Southeast
☐ Southwest
☐ West

Appendix E: Field Test Survey Questions

Critical Success Factors in Enterprise Resource Planning
Implementation in U.S. Manufacturing

1. Please provide any suggestions or comments regarding
the clarity or relevance of terms and definitions identified in
the survey.

(text box)

2. Please outline any areas where the survey instructions or
the questions can be improved.

(text box)

Appendix F: Reflexive Journal

11-21-17
Set up notifications in Google Scholar to receive notifications for journal articles regarding Delphi studies that use critical success factors in small- and medium-sized manufacturing organizations.

12-29-17
Reduced anticipated sample size of expert panel from 75 to 50 after working with dissertation chair and concluding that 75 participants would extend the research timeline.

1-12-18
In performing the literature review, identified a 75% threshold used to establish consensus in Round 2 and Round 3.

2-5-18
Changed conceptual framework from the DeLone and McLean Information Systems Success Model to the Critical Success Factor Framework after review and feedback from my second dissertation committee member.

3-27-18
To ensure internal consistency and reliability of instrument, incorporated Cronbach's alpha through the use of SPSS.

4-23-18
To test for face and content validity, switched from a pilot study to a field test.

5-17-18
Modified review process to only send my dissertation chair researcher's thoughts and revisions based on feedback instead of revising entire sections and/or chapters.

7-26-18
Made the following changes per IRB feedback:

- …added a note to the LinkedIn invitation and to the informed consent form stating that subsequent rounds are only open to participants that participated in previous rounds.
- …added a note to the informed consent form stating that the results of the study will be sent to the LinkedIn moderator of the group to post for review.
- …removed research jargon from all participant-facing documents (i.e. qualitative modified Delphi study)
- …added inclusion criteria to the informed consent form.
- …added the time period for each round of the study to the invitation and the informed consent form.
- …added the following statement to the Voluntary Nature of the Study section to the informed consent form: "If you have a relationship with the researcher and decide to decline or discontinue participation in the study, your relationship with the researcher will not be negatively impacted."
- …added the following statement to the informed consent form: "You may keep or print a copy of this consent form for future reference."

8-10-18
Made the following changes per IRB feedback:
- …created separate LinkedIn invitations for each round of the Delphi study.

9-15-18
Made an adjustment in demographic ordinal variable analysis to use frequency counts and percentages and the mode instead of median, mode, and range.

10-1-18
Sent my Round 1 survey data and Round 2 survey to Dr. Heitner to review and audit.

10-16-18
Sent Round 2 survey data to Dr. Heitner and made an adjustment to remove the median score as the second measure of consensus resulting in eight critical success factors moving to Round 3.

11-28-18
Because there was high consensus for all eight critical success factors in Round 3; increased the cutoff to 90% to answer the primary research question and sub-questions.

Appendix G: LinkedIn Group Messaging for Subsequent Rounds

Second Round Letter of Participation in Delphi Study

Dear ERP manufacturing consultant,

You have been invited to take part in the second round of a research study about critical success factors in Enterprise Resource Planning (ERP) implementations in the United States. The second round is only open to participants that participated in Round 1 of the study. This study is being conducted by Justin Goldston, who is a doctoral student at Walden University. You may already know the researcher as a Senior Management Consultant, but this study is separate from that role.

The purpose of this Delphi study is to identify a consensus among a panel of ERP manufacturing consultants as to the desirability and feasibility of critical success factors in ERP implementations in the United States. The study will involve at least three rounds of data collection and analysis.

To be eligible for the study, you should meet the following criteria:

a) have at least five years of experience implementing ERP applications
b) perform ERP implementations in the United States
c) perform ERP implementations in the industrial or manufacturing sector
d) perform ERP implementations for small- and medium-sized enterprises (firms that employ fewer than 500 employees).

If you would like to participate in the study, please select the following link: https://www.SurveyMonkey/r/erpcriticalsuccessfactors2

You may ask any questions you have now by contacting the researcher via ████████████████████ or ██████████████

Thank you for your consideration, and I look forward to your response in building on the ERP body of knowledge.

(Private information, e.g., phone numbers and email addresses, were redacted to retain privacy of the noted entities.)

Third Round Letter of Participation in Delphi Study

Dear ERP Manufacturing consultant,

You have been invited to take part in the third round of a research study about critical success factors in Enterprise Resource Planning (ERP) implementations in the United States. The third round is only open to participants that participated in Round 2 of the study. This study is being conducted by Justin Goldston, who is a doctoral student at Walden University. You may already know the researcher as a Senior Management Consultant, but this study is separate from that role.

The purpose of this Delphi study is to identify a consensus among a panel of ERP manufacturing consultants as to the desirability and feasibility of critical success factors in ERP implementations in the United States. The study will involve at least three rounds of data collection and analysis.

To be eligible for the study, you should meet the following criteria:

a) have at least five years of experience implementing ERP applications
b) perform ERP implementations in the United States
c) perform ERP implementations in the industrial or manufacturing sector
d) perform ERP implementations for small- and medium-sized enterprises (firms that employ fewer than 500 employees).

If you would like to participate in the study, please select the following link:
https://www.SurveyMonkey/r/erpcriticalsuccessfactors3

You may ask any questions you have now by contacting the researcher via ▮▮▮▮▮▮▮▮▮▮ or ▮▮▮▮▮▮▮.

Thank you for your consideration, and I look forward to your response in building on the ERP body of knowledge.

(Private information, e.g., phone numbers and email addresses, were redacted to retain privacy of the noted entities.)

Appendix H: Informed Consent Form

Dear Participant,

You have been invited to take part in a research study about critical success factors in Enterprise Resource Planning (ERP) implementations in the United States. This form is part of a process called 'informed consent' to allow you to understand this study before deciding whether or not to participate.

This study is being conducted by me, Justin Goldston, a doctoral student at Walden University. You may already know me as a Senior Management Consultant, but this study is separate from that role.

To be eligible for the study, you should meet the following criteria:

a) have at least five years of experience implementing ERP applications
b) perform ERP implementations in the United States
c) perform ERP implementations in the industrial or manufacturing sector
d) perform ERP implementations for small- and medium-sized enterprises (firms that employ fewer than 500 employees)

Background Information

The purpose of this Delphi study is to identify a consensus among a panel of ERP manufacturing consultants as to the desirability and feasibility of critical success factors in ERP implementations in the United States. The study will involve multiple rounds of data collection and analysis.

Procedures

If you agree to be in this study, each round of the survey should take approximately 5 minutes to complete. In the first round, you will be asked to rate critical success factors, while being allowed to add additional critical success factors. Also, you will also be asked demographic questions in Round 1. In Round 2, after evaluating the results, you will then be asked to rate the desirability and feasibility of the critical success factors using a Likert-type scale. Round 2 will only be open to participants that participated in Round 1. Based on the results of the second round, in the third round, if you participated in the first two rounds, you will be asked to rate the critical success factors with the highest desirability and feasibility until consensus is identified. If consensus is not reached in Round 3, subsequent rounds of rating will follow until a consensus of 75% is achieved. All rounds will be open for a period of two weeks. At the conclusion of the study, a page summary of the results will be sent to the LinkedIn moderator of this group to post for your review.

Voluntary Nature of the Study

This study is voluntary. You are free to accept or reject the invitation. Once the survey is submitted, it cannot be withdrawn due to your anonymous participation. You can decide to withdraw your consent and stop participating in the study at any time. If you have a relationship with the researcher and decide to decline or discontinue participation in the study, your relationship with the researcher will not be negatively impacted.

Risks and Benefits of Being in the Study

Being in this type of study involves some risk of the minor discomforts that can be encountered in everyday life. While there may not be a direct benefit to your participation, the potential benefit to this study will be to build upon the body of knowledge of the ERP consulting practice to better support clients in the United States.

Compensation

Participants will not be compensated for participating in this study.

Anonymity

The participants and their responses will be kept anonymous. No identifying information will be collected for this study, and the researcher will not collect participants' names or other identifying information. The researcher will not use your personal information for any purposes outside of this research project. The survey will be administered through SurveyMonkey with the site set not to collect Internet protocol (IP) addresses. Also, the researcher will not collect information such as your name on anything else that could identify you in the study reports.

SurveyMonkey is a secure online survey provider that institutes data collection, storage, and security measures that protect against unauthorized access on their website. SurveyMonkey will not use these data for any purpose. Data will be kept for a period of five years, as required by the university.

Contacts and Questions

You may ask any questions you have now. Or if you have any questions later, you may contact the researcher via justin.goldston@█████████ or █████████████; my dissertation chair, Dr. Keri Heitner, via ███████████ ██████████████; or if you have questions regarding your rights as a participant, you may contact Walden University's IRB at IRB@██████████.

The approval number for this study is 09-17-18-0643463 and it expires on September 16th, 2019.

You may keep or print a copy of this consent form for future reference.

Obtaining Your Consent

If you feel you understand the study well enough, please indicate your consent by clicking this link █ █████ .

(Private information, e.g., phone numbers and email addresses, were redacted to retain privacy of the noted entities.)

Appendix I: SurveyMonkey Privacy Policy

The SurveyMonkey privacy policy is located at this URL. This URL is provided to avoid any potential of plagiarism of word-for-word legal notification at the time of the research study in this copyrighted publication.

https://www.SurveyMonkey/mp/legal/privacy-policy/

Appendix J: Round 1

Non-narrative Results Summary

Critical Success Factor	(1) Highly Undesirable n (%)	(2) Undesirable n (%)	(3) Neutral n (%)	(4) Desirable n (%)	(5) Highly Desirable n (%)	Top two responses (percent)
1. Cultural change readiness	0 (0.00)	2 (3.92)	3 (5.88)	17 (33.33)	29 (56.86)	90.19
2. Top management support and commitment	1 (1.96)	0 (0.00)	0 (0.00)	4 (7.84)	46 (90.20)	98.04
3. Knowledge capacity production network	1 (1.96)	2 (3.92)	13 (25.49)	26 (50.98)	9 (17.65)	68.63
4. Minimum customization	3 (5.88)	3 (5.88)	13 (25.49)	16 (31.37)	16 (31.37)	62.74
5. Legacy systems support	1 (1.96)	9 (17.65)	22 (43.14)	18 (35.29)	1 (1.96)	37.25
6. ERP fit with the organization	0 (0.00)	0 (0.00)	3 (5.88)	19 (37.25)	29 (56.86)	94.11
7. Local vendor's partnership	3 (5.88)	5 (9.80)	24 (47.06)	19 (37.25)	0 (0.00)	37.25
8. Detailed cost	1 (1.96)	1 (1.96)	9 (17.65)	38 (74.51)	2 (3.92)	78.43
9. Business process re-engineering	0 (0.00)	0 (0.00)	2 (3.92)	22 (43.14)	27 (52.94)	96.08
10. Quality management	0 (0.00)	0 (0.00)	0 (0.00)	18 (35.29)	33 (64.71)	100.00
11. Risk Management	0 (0.00)	2 (3.92)	6 (11.96)	28 (54.90)	15 (29.41)	84.31
12. Detailed data migration plan readiness	0 (0.00)	0 (0.00)	0 (0.00)	28 (54.90)	23 (45.10)	100.00
13. Measurable goals	0 (0.00)	2 (3.92)	11 (21.57)	24 (47.06)	14 (27.45)	74.51
14. Small internal team of the best employees	0 (0.00)	3 (5.88)	3 (5.88)	10 (19.61)	35 (68.63)	88.24
15. Open and transparent communication	0 (0.00)	0 (0.00)	3 (5.88)	23 (45.10)	25 (49.02)	94.12
16. Base point analysis	0 (0.00)	2 (3.92)	25 (49.02)	18 (35.29)	6 (11.76)	47.05
17. Moral maintenance	0 (0.00)	3 (5.88)	6 (11.76)	30 (58.82)	12 (23.53)	82.35
18. Contingency plans	0 (0.00)	0 (0.00)	2 (3.92)	41 (80.39)	8 (15.69)	96.08
19. ERP success documentation	0 (0.00)	2 (3.92)	16 (31.37)	26 (50.98)	7 (13.73)	64.71
20. User feedback usage	0 (0.00)	0 (0.00)	10 (19.61)	24 (47.06)	17 (33.33)	80.39
21. Maximum potential usage	0 (0.00)	2 (3.92)	7 (13.73)	28 (54.90)	14 (27.45)	82.35
22. Results measurement	0 (0.00)	0 (0.00)	21 (41.18)	22 (43.14)	8 (15.69)	58.83

Appendix K: Permission to Produce Existing Figures

EMERALD PUBLISHING LIMITED LICENSE TERMS AND CONDITIONS

Jan 08, 2018

This Agreement between Justin Goldston ("You") and Emerald Publishing Limited ("Emerald Publishing Limited") consists of your license details and the terms and conditions provided by Emerald Publishing Limited and Copyright Clearance Center.

License Number	4264230084531
License date	Jan 08, 2018
Licensed Content Publisher	Emerald Publishing Limited
Licensed Content Publication	Journal of Enterprise Information Management
Licensed Content Title	Critical success factors in enterprise resource planning implementation
Licensed Content Author	Raafat George Saade, Harshjot Nijher
Licensed Content Date	Feb 8, 2016
Licensed Content Volume	29
Licensed Content Issue	1
Type of Use	Dissertation/Thesis
Requestor type	Academic
Author of requested content	No
Portion	Figures/table/illustration
Number of figures/tables	1
Will you be translating?	No
Format	Electronic
Geographic Rights	World rights
Order Reference Number	
Requestor Location	Justin Goldston 139 Colorado Ave
	LITTLESTOWN, PA 17340 United States Attn: Justin Goldston
Publisher Tax ID	GB 665359306
Billing Type	Invoice
Billing Address	Justin Goldston 139 Colorado Ave
	LITTLESTOWN, PA 17340 United States Attn: Justin Goldston
Total	0.00 USD
Terms and Conditions	

EMERALD PUBLISHING LIMITED ORDER DETAILS

Jan 19, 2018

This Agreement between ("You") and Emerald Publishing Limited ("Emerald Publishing Limited") consists of your order details and the terms and conditions provided by Emerald Publishing Limited and Copyright Clearance Center.

Order Number	501355551
Order date	Jan 17, 2018
Licensed Content Publisher	Emerald Publishing Limited
Licensed Content Publication	Internet Research: Electronic Networking Applications and Policy
Licensed Content Title	The value of online surveys
Licensed Content Author	Joel R. Evans, Anil Mathur
Licensed Content Date	Apr 1, 2005
Licensed Content Volume	15
Licensed Content Issue	2
Type of Use	Dissertation/Thesis
Requestor type	Academic
Author of requested content	No
Portion	Figures/table/illustration
Number of figures/tables	1
Will you be translating?	No
Format	Electronic
Geographic Rights	World rights
Order Reference Number	
Requestor Location	Justin Goldston 139 Colorado Ave
	LITTLESTOWN, PA 17340 United States Attn: Justin Goldston
Publisher Tax ID	GB 665359306
Billing Type	Invoice
Billing Address	Justin Goldston 139 Colorado Ave
	LITTLESTOWN, PA 17340 United States Attn: Justin Goldston
Total	0.00 USD
Terms and Conditions	

TERMS AND CONDITIONS

These URLs are provided to avoid any potential of plagiarism of word-for-word legal notification at the time of the research study in this copyrighted publication.

Emerald Publishing

Terms and Conditions

http://www.emeraldgrouppublishing.com/products/subs/terms.htm

Permission to Publish

http://www.emeraldgrouppublishing.com/licensing/permissions.htm

**ELSEVIER LICENSE
TERMS AND CONDITIONS**

Jan 13, 2018

This Agreement between Justin Goldston ("You") and Elsevier ("Elsevier") consists of your license details and the terms and conditions provided by Elsevier and Copyright Clearance Center.

License Number	4267330853132
License date	Jan 13, 2018
Licensed Content Publisher	Elsevier
Licensed Content Publication	Journal of Cleaner Production
Licensed Content Title	Sustainable enterprise resource planning: imperatives and research directions
Licensed Content Author	Abdoulmohammad Gholamzadeh Chofreh,Feybi Ariani Goni,Awaluddin Mohamed Shaharoun,Syuhaida Ismail,Jiří Jaromír Klemeš
Licensed Content Date	May 15, 2014
Licensed Content Volume	71
Licensed Content Issue	n/a
Licensed Content Pages	9
Start Page	139
End Page	147
Type of Use	reuse in a thesis/dissertation
Portion	figures/tables/illustrations
Number of figures/tables/illustrations	1
Format	electronic
Are you the author of this Elsevier article?	No
Will you be translating?	No
Original figure numbers	Fig. 2. Sustainability research in value chain
Title of your thesis/dissertation	Building Consensus for Critical Success in ERP Implementation in US Manufacturing
Expected completion date	Jul 2018
Estimated size (number of pages)	210
Requestor Location	Justin Goldston 139 Colorado Ave
	LITTLESTOWN, PA 17340 United States Attn: Justin Goldston
Publisher Tax ID	98-0397604
Total	0.00 USD

**ELSEVIER LICENSE
TERMS AND CONDITIONS**

Feb 07, 2018

This Agreement between Justin Goldston ("You") and Elsevier ("Elsevier") consists of your license details and the terms and conditions provided by Elsevier and Copyright Clearance Center.

License Number	4283970631469
License date	Feb 07, 2018
Licensed Content Publisher	Elsevier
Licensed Content Publication	International Journal of Project Management
Licensed Content Title	A new framework for determining critical success/failure factors in projects
Licensed Content Author	Walid Belassi, Oya Iemeli Tukel
Licensed Content Date	Jun 1, 1996
Licensed Content Volume	14
Licensed Content Issue	3
Licensed Content Pages	11
Start Page	141
End Page	151
Type of Use	reuse in a thesis/dissertation
Portion	figures/tables/illustrations
Number of figures/tables/illustrations	1
Format	electronic
Are you the author of this Elsevier article?	No
Will you be translating?	No
Original figure numbers	Table 2
Title of your thesis/dissertation	Building Consensus for Critical Success in ERP Implementation in US Manufacturing
Expected completion date	Jul 2018
Estimated size (number of pages)	210
Requestor Location	Justin Goldston 139 Colorado Ave LITTLESTOWN, PA 17340 United States Attn: Justin Goldston
Publisher Tax ID	98-0397604
Total	0.00 USD
Terms and Conditions	

These URLs are provided to avoid any potential of plagiarism of word-for-word legal notification at the time of the research study in this copyrighted publication.

Elsevier Publishing

Terms and Conditions

https://www.elsevier.com/legal/elsevier-website-terms-and-conditions

Permission to Publish

https://www.elsevier.com/about/policies/copyright/permissions

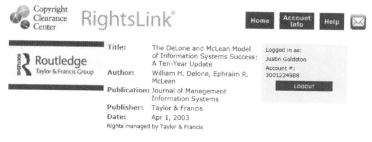

Thesis/Dissertation Reuse Request

Taylor & Francis is pleased to offer reuses of its content for a thesis or dissertation free of charge contingent on resubmission of permission request if work is published.

Taylor & Francis

These URLs are provided to avoid any potential of plagiarism of word-for-word legal notification at the time of the research study in this copyrighted publication.

Terms and Conditions

https://www.tandfonline.com/terms-and-conditions

Permission to Publish

https://www.routledge.com/info/permissions

INDEX

CURRICULUM VITAE

Justin Goldston, Ph.D.
CSCP, CTL, PLS, PSM
justin.goldston@academiaworldwide.com

Statement of Teaching Philosophy

My philosophy of teaching is based on past management consulting experience and to bring that knowledge into the classroom. After being mentored by various astute instructors, as well as established business leaders, it is my time to pay it forward. The most valuable information I can provide is the knowledge garnered over a decade of consulting within a business environment that is an ever-evolving landscape. Though some of these experiences, tools, skills, traits, and characteristics can be found in books or articles, my ultimate goal is to prepare future leaders for encountered nuances as they progress throughout their careers.

I am a believer communication and collaboration are a foundation of any learning experience. Factoring in an online environment, these two metrics are amplified for a concise and transparent delivery of course material to students. Due to my passion for the business management and leadership fields and my goal to get more future professionals interested in these fields, I keep each student engaged throughout the course with my own desire to build a foundation for the student's success academically, as well as in their future careers.

Students view the instructor as the facilitator and a provider of information as it pertains to coursework with extensive experience in both face-to-face and online settings. I have consulted for dozens of organizations spanning various industries, thus am able to incorporate real-life case studies from the experience to provide a practitioner's lens of the topics.

I strive to provide detailed explanations of the marks on assignments to enable the students to build their knowledge and skills as the course progresses. Being innovative is how I connect with students … it's a call to action … using video announcements, engaging discussion, and periodic town-hall sessions where the learners share their ideas and concerns within a solidified group. My objective is to connect with students on a personal level. My teaching skills and mentoring experience, as well as knowledge of current research as an instructor, I am able to maintain a constant presence as a Subject Matter Expert in the classroom, which in turn increases student success and retention. By creating a collaborative environment and cohort among students, this leads to individual student success.

Higher Education / Academic Experience

Adjunct Faculty
2018 – present
Aurora University, Aurora, IL

- Review / update course syllabi to achieve course outcomes and measurements within the MBA program.
- Perform audits of course content based on research of the latest trends in Operations Management and Supply Chain Management.
- Record weekly asynchronous sessions to outline weekly objectives and deliverables.

Courses taught in Moodle:

MBA-6030 Leadership & Organizational Behavior: This course introduces students to an advanced treatment of the behavioral role of the leader interacting with others within the organization. It offers a critical review of leadership and human behavior and addresses those behavioral concepts that influence such factors as group dynamics, interpersonal relations, and ultimately, organizational effectiveness.

MBA-6610 Leading Organizational Development: In today's global marketplace, the organizations that thrive are the ones that anticipate change and create new adaptations to their business model. Creativity is the key to finding new opportunities and establishing a competitive advantage through collaborative teams and the use of organizational alliances and strategic partnerships. The three subsections are (1) creating competitive advantage through teamwork (2) global alliances and partners and (3) emerging topics.

Adjunct Faculty
2018 – present
North Carolina Wesleyan College, Rocky Mount, NC

- Responsible for creating course syllabi for each course.
- Provided timely and constructive feedback to students to improve on coursework and apply to their respective professional backgrounds.
- Ensured student success by providing support and collaboration with student advising and academic teams.

Courses taught in Jenzabar:

BUS-309 Principles of Transportation; Examines the forms of transportation and the institutional factors that influence transportation decisions; regulation, public policy, and other governmental variables reviewed in detail. All modes of transportation will be considered: trucking, highways, mass transit, airlines, maritime, railroads, and pipelines.

BUS-312 Global Logistics: This course examines the global transportation of goods with an emphasis on analyzing, forwarding and selecting the proper mode of transportation consistent with the goods being transported. This course will provide in-depth learning on the proper logistics activities and the flow of goods including customer service and order processing, warehousing, materials handling, inventory concepts, Logistics Information Systems and traffic, and transportation. Also covered will be the importance of documentation, boycotts, the role of the third party in financing, embargoes, and NAFTA and other consortiums. Upon the completion of this course, the student will be able to coordinate and arrange global transportation of goods.

BUS-451 Supply Chain Management: The concepts and methods in this course are associated with viewing organizations as integrated systems and members of integrated supply chains. The approaches to achieve a competitive advantage through planning, organizing, leading and controlling will be reviewed. The application of quantitative techniques to organizational and supply chain management problems will also be reviewed.

BUS-455 Contemporary Logistics: This course involves managing the logistics component of the supply chain practice that is concerned with the forward and reverse flows, as well as the storage of goods and services in the business environment. A strong focus on the management of goods and services from the point of origin to the point of utilization will be demonstrated in this course. Also, the development of plans,
implementation and control measures will be reviewed in this course.

Associate Professor
2017 - Present
The Jack Welch Management Institute, Herndon, VA

- Responsible for providing substantive and timely feedback within the Executive MBA program. Recorded weekly asynchronous sessions to outline weekly objectives and deliverables.
- Hosted synchronous sessions throughout the term to address student questions. Assisted the Dean and Faculty and Course Lead on evaluating course objectives.

Courses taught in Blackboard:

JWI-550 Operations Management: This course explores such topics as process mapping, project management, operations design, quality improvement, inventory and supply chain management, Six Sigma and lean operations techniques, forecasting and planning, and sustainability.

Adjunct Faculty
2017 - Present
Southern New Hampshire University, Hooksett, NH

Courses taught in Desire2Learn (Brightspace):

QSO-330 Supply Chain Management: Focuses on effective supply chain strategies for companies that operate globally with emphasis on how to plan and integrate supply chain components into a coordinated system. Students are exposed to concepts and models important in supply chain planning with emphasis on key tradeoffs and phenomena. The course introduces and utilizes key tactics such as risk pooling and inventory placement, integrated planning and collaboration, and information sharing.

QSO-455 Integrated Supply Chain Management: Examines key issues associated with design and management of supply chains. Students examine modern supply chain management practices. Emphasis is on exploration of how to integrate suppliers, factories, stores, and warehouses so products are distributed to customers in right quantity / at right time. A key topic area is service logistics and distribution component of the supply chain.

QSO-415 Trends in Operations Management: This course focuses on contemporary topics in operations management. Examples of topics that will be explored included assessing and managing disruptive change, agile project management, automation, innovation, and technology trends.

QSO-300 Operations Management: This course is an introduction to the operations function, which is responsible for the creation of goods and services of the organization. Students will learn the concepts and techniques used in managing operations in manufacturing and service organizations.

QSO-322 Logistics Management: This course provides an overview of the field of logistics including its nature, scope, and process, including logistics management functions and the interrelationships among strategic support and operational logistics. Students examine the logistics functions of business involved in the movement and storage of supplies, work-in-progress, and finished goods. Additionally, it explores the trade-offs between cost and service and the purchase and supply of raw materials.

QSO-425 Reverse Logistics: Provides an overview of today's best practices in reverse logistics. An application perspective is examined in manufacturing, retail, and military. Students examine nature, scope, practices, procedures, and processes of adding a reverse logistics operations center to a forward logistics supply chain.

Doctoral Mentor
2016 - Present
Walden University, Minneapolis, MN

- Supervised and mentored a group of 73 new PhD students on best practices, lessons learned and guidance.
- Increased the retention rate of first-year PhD students at the university.
- Led a study to uncover the reasons why online PhD programs incur high dropout rates.
- Integral in working with students on selecting dissertation topics, constructing problem statements and research questions.
- Established techniques and methods to analyze qualitative and quantitative data during course work and dissertation phases of student's PhD program.

Industry and Professional Experience

2018 – present
Senior Consultant
Ultra Consultants

- Instrumental as the Change Manager for cloud-based implementation projects by aligning continuous improvement initiatives with strategic business objectives by making recommendations to modify processes to improve operational efficiencies.
- Designed marketing survey research questionnaires, provided sample sizes and checked survey results using Statistical Analytics Software (SAS) for the organization.
- Assisted in developing and re-engineering the organization's implementation methodology as a member of the Center of Excellence.
- Led bi-weekly webinars on concepts such as supply chain integration, blockchain integration, cloud enablement, and best practices in ERP selection and implementation.

2015 – 2017
Senior Management Consultant
Plex Systems, Troy, MI

- Conducted instructor-led training sessions on Procure to Pay, Order to Cash, and Plan to Produce for clients in various industries.
- Created, defined, and led forums with key stakeholders enhancing communication, collaboration, and global alignment related to business practices, policies, and processes.
- Assessed business strategies of clients, including analysis of working capital, process workflows, financial inefficiencies and new business opportunities.
- Collaborated with Education Services department to re-engineer onboarding process to enable employees to utilize accelerated leading, coaching and mentoring.
- Consulted on industry best practices, the importance of measurement and standard methodologies through the utilization of academic research and creation of key performance indicators (KPI's).

2012 - 2015
Senior Consultant / Project Manager
Infor Global, New York, NY

- Guided a consulting team through transition from a waterfall to an Agile implementation methodology for the installation of SyteLine at Intel.
- Directed change management initiatives in Project Manager/Consultant role to plan, schedule and execute implementations / mitigating risk through project life.
- Provided synchronous and asynchronous training sessions to supply chain professionals on topics of supply chain management, operations management, materials requirements planning (MRP), Distribution Requirements Planning (DRP), Sales & Operations Planning (S&OP), and Vendor Managed Inventory (VMI).

- Provided advisory services to firms to guide decision-making on startup opportunities, mergers, and other financial opportunities.
- Instituted Six Sigma and Lean methodologies for process improvement, saving manufacturing clients an average of $100,000 annually.
- Developed / monitored project plans during pre-sales / implementation life cycles resulting in identification of key issues, approaches, and mitigation strategies.
- Deployed a Sales and Operations Planning (S&OP) methodology for a heavy machinery manufacturer.
- Increased forecasting accuracy by 30%, stockout reduction by 25% and a fill rate of 98%.

2006 – 2012
Senior Business Consultant - Project Manager
IBS, Folsom, CA

- Assisted in development of a Customer Relationship Management (CRM) module for IBS Enterprise.
- Established Search Engine Optimization (SEO) project, resulting in a 51% increase in online sales.
- Led global manufacturing re-engineering project for a mining equipment manufacturer with sites in the United States, Canada, Chile, Switzerland, and Finland.
- Reduced overall set-up times (70%); eliminating queue times with introduction of work cells on shop floor.
- Spearheaded the successful coordination of a Collaborative Planning Forecasting and Replenishment (CPFR) program for pet food manufacturer working with retailers (e.g., PetCo, PetSmart, Tractor Supply).
- Reduced stockouts by 60%, excess inventory by 25% and inventory carrying costs by 50%.

Entrepreneurial Experience

2016 - Present
Academia Worldwide
Gettysburg, PA

- Served as external evaluator to review proposal for DBA program seeking accreditation from Massachusetts Department of Higher Education (MDHE).
- Lead academic consultant that specializes in higher education assistance for undergraduate, graduate, and PhD students in online / brick-&-mortar environments.
- Provide undergraduate students with university survival and financial independence support throughout their undergraduate journey.
- Established approach to prepare Master-level students with tools to advance careers; worked closely with universities place new upper-level graduates in firms such as Under Armour and Intel.
- Assist new graduate students with support to transition back into school in an online environment.
- Support PhD students through all phases of their dissertation by providing APA, premise, prospectus, proposal, and editing services.
- Deliver career planning for students (all levels).

2012 - Present
Provision Consulting Worldwide
Gettysburg, PA

- Principal for a management consulting firm that specializes in small / medium enterprise vertical assisting startups to established firms.
- Provide leadership, management, marketing, sales and supply chain/logistics services from near-shoring decisions to on-premise and cloud ERP selection for firms across the USA; provide SME experience in fields of industrial engineering, enterprise applications,

business process integration/re-engineering, mergers and acquisitions, and supply chain management.

- Strategic verticals supported encompass manufacturing, distribution, retail, financial services, healthcare and higher education.
- Assisted organizations in streamlining their business operations, increasing their profitability and transforming their organizations into more organic work environments.

Formal Education

- 2019, Ph.D., Management Leadership and Organizational Change, Walden University, Minneapolis, MN
- 2014, Master of Professional Studies, Supply Chain Management, Pennsylvania State University, University Park, PA
- 2006, Bachelor of Science, Supply Chain Management, North Carolina Agricultural and Technical State University, Greensboro, NC

Licenses and Certificates

- 2019, Certified, Blockchain, Cornell University
- 2018, Professional Scrum Master, The Scrum Alliance
- 2018, Certified, Lean Six Sigma Green Belt, Six Sigma Global Institute
- 2014, Professional Designation in Logistics and Supply Chain Management (PLS), American Production and Inventory Control Society (APICS)
- 2014, Certified, Transportation and Logistics (CTL), American Production and Inventory Control Society (APICS)
- 2013, Certified, Supply Chain Management, Pennsylvania State University

- 2012, Certified, Supply Chain Professional (CSCP), American Production and Inventory Control Society (APICS)

Educational Training

- 05/18, BP 200 - Foundations of Online Course Delivery, Aurora University
- 05/18, MT 204 - Faculty Orientation to Moodle for Master Courses, Aurora University
- 12/17, Agile Instructional Design, Allen Interactions, Inc.
- 11/17, How to Design and Deliver Training Programs, Instructional Design: Needs Analysis, Toister Performance Solutions
- 11/17, Instructional Design for Adult Learners
- 11/17, ADJ-185 Brightspace Training for Graduate and Undergraduate Faculty, Southern New Hampshire University
- 10/17, JWI000-1178 New Faculty Certification, Jack Welch Management Institute
- 10/17, ADJ-101 New Adjunct Faculty Training, Southern New Hampshire University
- 04/17, Best Practices for Delivering a Course Online, Northern Illinois University - Faculty Development and Instructional Design Center
- 04/17, Designing Exemplary Online Courses in Blackboard, Northern Illinois University - Faculty Development and Instructional Design Center
- 04/17, Online Couse Activities and Student Engagement, Northern Illinois University - Faculty Development and Instructional Design Center
- 05/17, Creating Authentic Experiences for Your Online Course, Northern Illinois University - Faculty Development and Instructional Design Center
- 05/17, Tips for Teaching Online in Blackboard, Online Learning Consortium

- 01/17, Supporting New Online Learners, Online Learning Consortium
- 01/17, Facilitating Group Work Online, Online Learning Consortium
- 01/17, Increasing Interaction and Engagement, Online Learning Consortium
- Association for Supervision and Curriculum Development (ASCD)
- 12/16, Get in the Game: The Magic Circle of the Gamified Classroom, Association for Supervision and Curriculum Development (ASCD)
- 12/16, Steps to Becoming a Highly Effective Teacher, Association for Supervision and Curriculum Development (ASCD)
- 12/16, Balanced Leadership for Powerful Learning, Learning Targets, Association for Supervision and Curriculum Development (ASCD)
- 10/16, Helping Students Aim for Understanding in Today's Lesson, Association for Supervision and Curriculum Development (ASCD)
- 09/16, Peer Coaching: Pathways for Teaching Excellence, and Student Achievement, Association for Supervision and Curriculum Development (ASCD)

Business and Technical Training

- 02/17, Professional Services Consulting Fundamentals Workshop, PS Principles
- 07/16, Scrum: The Basics, The Scrum Alliance
- 07/16, Scrum: Advanced, The Scrum Alliance
- 07/16, Transitioning from Waterfall to Agile Project Management, The Scrum Alliance
- 01/16, Six Sigma Foundations, Acuity Institute
- 01/16, Six Sigma: Green Belt, Acuity Institute
- 01/16, Six Sigma: Black Belt, Acuity Institute

Journal Article Reviewer

- 2018 – present, International Journal of Responsible Management Education
- 2016 – present, Academy of International Business
- 2016 – present, Academy of Management
- 2015 – present, European Academy of Management

Scholarly and Professional Presentations

Goldston, J. (2019). Blockchaining Day: The Future is Here. TEDxCocoaBeach, Cocoa Beach, FL.

Goldston, J. (2019). Web 3.0: The Blockchain Effect. TEDxCalvinCollege, Grand Rapids, MI.

Goldston, J. (2019). The Societal Impact of Blockchain Technologies. TEDxACU (Abilene Christian University), Abilene, TX.

Goldston, J. (2019). Why You Should Create Your Own Blockchain. TEDxNorthParkUniversity, Chicago, IL.

Goldston, J. (2019). How Blockchain will Positively Change Our Lives. TEDxRIT (Rochester Institute of Technology), Rochester, NY.

Goldston, J. (2017, March). Mitigating ERP Implementation Risk in SMEs: An Empirical View.

International Conference on Interdisciplinary Research Studies, Silver Spring, MD. Goldston, J. (2016). Residency Town Hall. Presented to first-year Walden University PhD Students.

Goldston, J. (2016). Deconstructing the Literature Review with the Literature Matrix. Presented to the Walden University PhD Dissertation Cohort.

Goldston, J. (2014). CPFR in Action. Presented to the Rutgers University MBA Program.

Goldston, J. (2014). Opportunities in Supply Chain Management and Business Consulting. Presented to the Morgan State University MBA Program.

Articles in which Cited

Satterfield, C. (2017). The cloud of IoT – what have you done in the last 60 seconds online?

Memberships and Affiliations

- 2016 – present, Organization Development Network
- 2016 – present, Society for Human Resource Management (SHRM)
- 2015 – present, Academy of Management (AOM)
- 2012 – present, American Society of Transportation & Logistics (AST&L)
- 2011 – present, Project Management Institute (PMI)
- 2011 – present, Association for Operations Management (APICS)

Community Service and Social Contributions

- 2016 – present, Member, Walden University Dissertation Cohort

Conferences Attended

- 03/17, Academy of Business Research Conference
- 05/16, Annual Strategic Alliance Management Congress
- 04/16, International Conference on Business Research and Management Practices
- 02/16, Strategic Business Management & Economic Research Conference

Residencies and Colloquia

- 10/18, Virtual Residency 4, Walden University
- 01/18, Washington D.C. Residency 3, Walden University
- 03/17, PhD Colloquia, International Conference on Interdisciplinary Research Studies
- 01/17, Virtual Residency 2, Walden University
- 03/16, Alexandria Residency 1, Walden University

Highly Competent Subject Areas

Software

- Evernote
- GoToMeeting
- Microsoft Office Suite
- NVivo
- Skype Zoom WebEx
- Statistical Package for the Social Sciences (SPSS)

Learning Management Systems

- Angel Blackboard
- Desire2Learn (D2L) eCollege
- Jenzabar
- Moodle
- Schoology uLearn

Subject Matter Expert

- Blockchain
- Business Strategy
- Consulting
- Lean Manufacturing
- Organizational Change
- Organizational Leadership
- Project Management
- Purchasing
- Six Sigma
- Statistics
- Supply Chain Management Operations Management
- Transportation and Logistics

Personal Attributes

- Highly qualified educator with over five years of teaching experience.
- Detail oriented professional with extensive senior level management experience.
- Apply a variety of teaching styles and adapt instruction to students with diverse learning styles. Ability to excel in a demanding, outcome-oriented, and dynamic work environment.
- Proven teaching strategies that promote student success.
- Skilled in many disciplines such as consulting, marketing and organizational leadership. Certified professional able to apply real world relevance to the classroom setting.
- Accomplished international management consulting professional and scholar-practitioner. Effective communication skills and a high level of attention to detail.
- Collaboration skills with peers to put teaching concepts and theories into practice. Enthusiasm for the subject matter exhibiting a willingness to learn and develop new skills. Ability to handle pressure and meet deadlines in any situation.
- Flexibility to teach a variety of courses based on academic and career backgrounds.

ABOUT THE AUTHOR

The author and seven-time TEDx speaker, Justin Goldston Ph.D., lives in Gettysburg, PA with his wife Melea. He has a Bachelor of Science degree in Supply Chain Management (North Carolina Agricultural and Technical State University, 2006), a Master's Degree in Supply Chain Management (Pennsylvania State University, 2014), and a Doctorate of Philosophy in Management, with a concentration in Leadership and Organizational Change (Walden University, 2019).

Dr. Goldston has held leadership roles within ERP vendors, while also adding his expertise in Project Management, Supply Chain Management, Lean Six Sigma and ERP to several manufacturing organizations around the world.

With deep domain experience in the field as well as his significant education, Dr. Goldston has taught Supply Chain Management, Project Management, and Operations Management as an Associate Professor at the undergraduate and Executive MBA levels, and has been a guest lecturer at Morgan State University and Rutgers University. Dr. Goldston also is a Professional Scrum Master, a Lean Six Sigma Green Belt, a Certified Supply Chain Professional, and holds a certificate in Blockchain from Cornell University.

SOCIAL MEDIA CONNECTIONS

Dr. Goldston can be contacted at:
justin.goldston@academiaworldwide.com

LinkedIn: www.Linkedin.com/in/justin-goldston

Academia Worldwide: http://academiaworldwide.com/

ABOUT THE BOOK

Enterprise Resource Planning (ERP) implementations can be costly for any company. While there are advantages to size and funding in larger businesses (500+ employees), there are critical success factors of the ERP process that small- to mid-size manufacturing (or other types of business organizations) can use to increase their rate of success for ERP. This *must-buy* book outlines research that targeted specific factors that increase any ERP implementation's success.

Critical success factors were identified, and ranked, by 50+ subject matter expert consultants in the ERP field in this study. These SMEs, all with more than five years of experience in implementing ERPs for manufacturers, provided a consensus for best-practices factors vital for consideration for the ERP implementation, before, during, and after the exercise. Critical factors (failure and success) are highlighted for the planning, process, and follow-up, with positive internal and external results from the executive (top-down) buy-in to the communications and transparency of the process to middle management and line employee stakeholders.

The vital points in the conclusion offer guidance to organizations, as well as ERP consultants, that are considering ERP implementation, even if the entity is not in the manufacturing industry. If you or your company is seriously considering an ERP project, this book is a required reading for industry intelligence and analytic insight.

Proceeds from this book will benefit *The Sydney Goldston Scholarship Foundation* to make the dreams for future leaders a reality. More information about the foundation can be found at: www.thesydneyfoundation.org

Made in the USA
Columbia, SC
05 September 2022